THE ABC's OF SELF-ESTEEM

A PRACTICAL APPROACH

Volume 1

BY

Curt Boudreaux, M.Ed.

THE ABC'S OF SELF-ESTEEM: A PRACTICAL APPROACH

PUBLISHED BY SYNERGY PRESS

ABITA SPRINGS, LOUISIANA

MANUFACTURED IN THE UNITED STATES OF AMERICA.

ISBN 1-889968-50-1

CONTENTS

DEDICATION

With much love and gratitude, this book is dedicated to the two most important women in my life:

My Mother, the late Margaret Baradell Boudreaux, who instilled in me the importance of an education and always said that I could accomplish anything I sincerely pursued. Her love, faith in God and belief in me were unwavering

and

My wife, Sue Oglesby Boudreaux, whose love, support and encouragement are unending and a constant source of inspiration. You are always there for me. In the words of the contemporary song by Celine Dion, "I'm everything I am because you love me."

ACKNOWLEDGMENTS

Special thanks and appreciation are expressed to the following people for their contributions:

Charlotte Riche, Executive Director, The Chamber of Commerce of Lafourche and the Bayou Region, for reading the manuscript draft and providing feedback. Know that I value and appreciate your friendship.

Mary Rabb, Guidance Counselor, Larose-Cut Off Junior High School for also reading the rough draft and giving feedback. I especially appreciate your efforts at such a busy time of year for you.

Tina Thomas, R.N., B.C.S.W., a fellow member of the New Orleans Chapter of the National Speakers Association and my "book buddy." You not only prodded me to commit to writing this book, but "held my feet to the fire" to see that it was done. Your insights and assistance with the manuscript were invaluable. You are a special friend.

Edmund Cappel, retired educator and my former English teacher, for editing the manuscript. I was a student in Edmund's English class during his first year of teaching at Thibodaux Junior High. He has been heard to remark on more than one occasion, "I still have nightmares about that class!"

Sharon Doucet, art teacher at South Lafourche High School and one of my former students, for creating and producing the illustrations.

Laura, Kelly and **Alison Champagne,** friends who not only did a super job of wife-sitting while this book was being written, but also while I was on the road and away from home. It gave me peace of mind to know that Sue was safe and in good hands.

Jim Hennig, Ph.D., CSP, CPAE, 1995-96 President of the National Speakers Association and a friend, for writing the Foreword. We are of kindred spirits and Jim and his wife, Coreen, are very special to me.

Og Mandino, CPAE, Congressman Billy Tauzin, Mark Kennedy, Elizabeth Jeffries, CSP, Carole Kennedy, Larry Koenig, Ph.D., Bobby Hebert, and Michael Mitchell for their endorsements.

Larry Williams, for designing the book cover and handling the details of publishing.

TESTIMONIALS

The ABC's of Self-Esteem: A Practical Approach
by Curt Boudreaux

"This very special book can change your life forever if you let it."

Og Mandino, CPAE
Author/Speaker
New Hampshire

"This should be required reading for every member of Congress. Part of the problem facing America today is the 'low esteem' people have for their leaders. By taking a few pointers from Curt Boudreaux, we could begin to restore trust in government and move our country forward. The book is filled with Cajun common sense!"

Congressman Billy Tauzin
Deputy Majority Whip
U.S. House of Representatives
Washington, D.C.

"Curt Boudreaux has in his book, **The ABC's of Self-Esteem: A Practical Approach,** given us a ready guide for becoming more positive, caring and contributing human beings. His sprinkling of humor and personal references add to the pleasure of reading and his challenge for each of us to grow and improve can make a difference if we follow the advice in this delightful book. As an educator of more than thirty years I can not only use the information as a reminder to myself, but also as I work with staff and students."

Carole Kennedy, President
National Association of Elementary School Principals
Columbia, Missouri

"In **The ABC's of Self-Esteem,** Curt Boudreaux creatively uses the alphabet to share powerful and thought provoking insights on self-esteem. You'll be drawn in with real life examples, affirmations and application exercises to help you change your thinking and your behavior. It's a course in self-esteem you won't want to miss!"

Elizabeth Jeffries, CSP
Speaker & Author
The Heart of Leadership: How to Inspire, Encourage and Motivate People to Follow You
Louisville, Kentucky

"Follow Curt Boudreaux's advice in this book and you will, no doubt, be positively changed. **The ABC's of Self-Esteem: A Practical Approach** effectively cuts through the fog many self-improvement authors tend to deliver. Curt's stories will make you laugh, inspire you and cause you to think."

Mark W. Kennedy
Senior Vice President
Cornerstone Health Management
Dallas, Texas

"If you are looking for a good book on self-esteem, then read Curt Boudreaux's book, **The ABC's of Self-Esteem.** It's enjoyable to read and anyone who tries out his belief building exercises couldn't help but both increase his self-esteem and the quality of his life as well."

Larry Koenig, Ph.D.
Founder/President, Up With Youth Company
Author of *Smart Discipline for the Classroom*
Baton Rouge, Louisiana

"This book is a winner. **The ABC's of Self-Esteem** is a book you won't put down until you have finished the alphabet as masterfully presented by Curt Boudreaux."

Michael A. Mitchell
Executive Director
Power of Positive Students Foundation
Myrtle Beach, South Carolina

"All of the topics discussed in **The ABC's of Self-Esteem** are truly needed to realize a successful and rewarding life. Confidence and self-esteem, which Curt covers in the book, are vital to achieve one's goals in today's world."

Bobby Hebert, Quarterback
Atlanta Falcons & New Orleans Saints
Alpharetta, Georgia

FOREWORD

Coreen and I were waiting in anticipation for the home-cooked authentic "New Orleans Gumbo" in our new found friends' home, Cathy and Ray Harris. We were watching for the arrival of Curt Boudreaux, the current president of the New Orleans Chapter of the National Speakers Association. (I was there as the visiting President of NSA.) We had no idea what had been the mission that prevented this seemingly unassuming and quiet man from joining us until later. He mentioned Kairos and prisons, but it was the evidence of an incredible spirit of humility and joy that impressed me most.

We found that the spirit of true service, beginning with this servant leader, permeated throughout the entire chapter. In the time since then, I have watched as he quietly and consistently fulfilled his duties as President and helped everyone recognize their true worth and contribution to the association as a whole.

As President of a 3600+ association that has as its members many great authors and speakers, I frequently am asked for my opinions or endorsements of many books. I see none that more fully align with the admonition that we so ardently support in NSA: "Walk Your Talk!"

The common sense, practical approach to building self-esteem obviously comes from one who has walked that journey. Curt's wit and enthusiasm take a serious matter and transform it into something uplifting and effective. Especially revealing and functional are the self-esteem exercises at the end of each chapter. I consider myself confident and of high self-esteem, but I fully intend to incorporate them into my own life creed.

As my wife and I would read together the chapters at night, we would invariably find a thought or story to tell one of our ten children about the following day to help them in this crucial area that can be the difference in lives that are happy and productive or ones that are fraught with failure.

This truly is a handbook to be read not once but as a valuable reference repeatedly. The fact that Curt and his Kairos group have been as effective as they are in the Louisiana Prison System speaks to the reality that it is never too late to learn or teach these valuable truths.

Winston Churchill said, "We make a living by what we get, we make a life by what we give." The lives that have been and will be touched through this one man's giving of his whole heart and soul with this book and his life truly will be worth more than gold and silver! I'm honored to be called your friend, Curt. God bless your work.

James F. Hennig, Ph.D, CSP, CPAE
President, National Speakers Association
Phoenix, Arizona

"People who feel good about themselves and who they are rarely engage in self-destructive or anti-social behavior."

INTRODUCTION

"A good name is more desirable than great riches, and high esteem, than gold and silver."

Proverbs 22:1

Society is faced with a myriad of problems today ranging from abuse in the home to violent crimes in the street. Reasons given for this decline are many and varied. A breakdown in family values, the high divorce rate, drug use and abuse, corruption in government, the educational system and loss of a work ethic are among those frequently mentioned.

A case can be made to suggest that these are not problems in and of themselves, but rather mere symptoms of a more deeply rooted problem — that of poor self-image and low self-esteem. People who feel good about themselves and who they are rarely engage in self-destructive or anti-social behavior.

Know that I am not naive enough to believe that simply building a positive self-image and raising self-esteem of the general populace alone will cure all of the ills of society. I do believe, however, that doing so can dramatically increase the chances for success in any endeavor and enhance the quality of life for all individuals.

Families, schools, communities, worksites, governments — all are made up of people. Each of these entities can and will be no better than the collective values, ethics, beliefs and esteem of its members. The whole is equal to the sum of its parts, for good or for bad. That's just the way it is.

The obvious conclusion to be considered at this point is that society can be improved by each individual taking the initiative to become a better person. I believe this to be true. As each individual grows and improves, society as a whole will get better, too. Imagine what would happen if every person improved only five percent! Individually it isn't very much. Collectively, it's an enormous amount and would undoubtedly make a decided difference. Significant positive change would take place in society.

I believe that building positive self-esteem is the logical starting point for meaningful change, both personally and socially. Therefore, the focus of this book will be directed to that end. An attempt has been made to keep it simple, easy to understand, enjoyable to read and practical to use. Reading this book will not change your life, but taking positive action will.

Improvement, however, will not come about simply by wishing and hoping. It will become a reality only when each individual makes a commitment to self-improvement and then follows through with positive action. Each of us must take responsibility for his/her own growth and development, for it is only ourselves that we can control.

A few more thoughts about self-image and self-esteem: although different, they are closely related. Self-image is the way we "see" ourselves based on information or feedback from other people. Self-esteem is the value we place on the picture of ourselves that we see. It's how we "feel" about the self we "see." The word esteem means to value, so self-esteem literally means the degree to which we value ourselves.

For the sake of convenience, I will refer only to self-esteem in the book. However, in most instances, the information applies to both since they are directly related. A positive self-image produces high self-esteem; a negative self-image results in low self-esteem. It's virtually impossible to deviate from this.

Each chapter is developed around a word corresponding to the letters of the alphabet. The twenty-six topic words relate in some fashion to self-esteem; however, liberties were taken occasionally in order to use a word for each letter. In my mind that is "author privilege."

It's not necessary to begin with Chapter 1. Each chapter is independent from the others, therefore, you may pick topics at random according to your interests. I like humor and have sprinkled liberal doses throughout the book. Sometimes I have squeezed it in amidst serious discussion. Please look for it and recognize it as such.

An opening quote sets the tone for the chapter. Credit is given to the author when it is known, however, those of unknown origin are identified as such.

An attitudinal affirmation is found at the end of each chapter. It is a conscious attempt to put specific information into the mind. A healthy portion of positive affirmation daily can help reprogram your subconscious mind and allow you to see yourself differently. Make up your own if you like, but do use them!

A belief building exercise and change producing action follow the affirmation. Action produces results and that is your goal. Little or nothing changes until some kind of action is taken. As the Nike slogan proclaims, "Just do it!"

Using the affirmations, exercises and positive actions contained in this book will plant the seeds that will ultimately make your self-esteem blossom and produce a positive change in your life. It's as easy as ABC. But it's your choice! Yours and yours alone! Since you've reached this point, I presume you have made the choice. Congratulations on your decision to improve your self-esteem and the quality of your life, and in the process, contribute to a better family, community and society!

A

"The mind is capable of holding literally thousands of thoughts during the course of a day, but only one at a time. That thought determines your attitude."

CHAPTER 1

Attitude

"You are where your thoughts have brought you. You will be tomorrow where your thoughts take you."

Ralph Waldo Emerson

A good attitude is an important ingredient for developing and maintaining self-esteem. Attitude is the way we view life and everything in it and how we respond to it. It is a feeling or emotion we have toward something or someone.

Attitude can be positive or negative depending upon our beliefs and our thoughts, for that is what determines it. A college professor posed this question to his class, "What do you think is the more serious problem facing our nation today – ignorance or apathy?" After a short pause a student in the back of the room jumped up and shouted, "I don't know and I don't care!" Then he looked at his classmates and said, "If you don't like my attitude, call 1-800-WHO CARES!" That's attitude, but certainly not a desirable one.

It all begins with what we believe and/or think. Our beliefs and thoughts determine our attitude which dictate how we feel about ourselves, others or a situation. These feelings, in turn, produce an action or behavior which always creates a consequence or result. The result then reinforces the original belief, thus making it stronger and more deeply rooted. This is illustrated in the "Behavior Cycle".

The Behavior Cycle

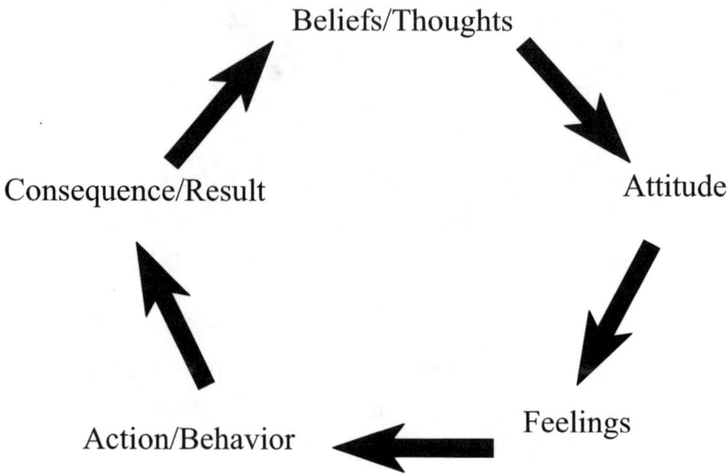

+ or -

Note that the cycle can be positive or negative depending upon the prevailing belief or thought. The mind is capable of holding literally thousands of thoughts during the course of a day, but only one at a time. If that thought is a positive one, then the flow of the Behavior Cycle will be positive thus producing desirable results. Similarly, a negative thought produces negative results.

What is crucial to remember is that we can choose our thoughts thereby choosing our attitude at any given time. Victor Frankel in his book, Man's Search For Meaning, says that "Man's greatest freedom is to be able to choose his attitude in any given set of circumstances." Therefore, attitude is a choice. What did you say when you woke up this morning — "Good morning, Lord!" or "Good Lord, it's morning?" That was your choice. A positive attitude may not solve all your problems, but it will annoy enough people to make it worth the effort!

Sometimes a traumatic experience can be a defining moment and change our attitude and outlook on life. As a youngster I maintained a high grade point average in school, but like many, did not handle the adolescent years very well. Academics became secondary and took a back seat to having fun. My grades dropped steadily between my freshmen and junior years.

During the summer of my junior year in high school, I worked for a company installing central air conditioning units. This job required working in extremely hot attics and then going into cool places. Doing this all summer finally took its toll. I was admitted to the hospital with double pneumonia and pleurisy the day before my senior year began. For three days the doctors did not know whether I would live or die. I was discharged after a two week hospital stay but missed the entire first month of my senior year.

With poor grades and weak study habits the previous year combined with current school absences, I was "struggling to come in last." To compound the problem, any kind of physical activity produced bronchitis and other illnesses. I was very sickly and in terrible condition. I realized at this point that I could not do manual labor and would need to consider going to college. I had little choice, so that is what I did.

This serious illness changed my attitude about school and was a pivotal point in my life. Although no one could have convinced me at the time, I came to realize that good fortune often comes disguised as adversity. I dread thinking about where I would be today had I not been seriously ill. Without a doubt I was on the wrong path and in need of a change in attitude. Thank God it came.

Eventually, however, our deeply imbedded beliefs control the cycle. We actually become what we believe about ourselves and act accordingly. In order to change our attitude or someone else's, it is necessary to change what is believed about ourselves or the other person. Beliefs will be discussed in the next chapter, but for the moment, review the Behavior Cycle to see the pattern.

A good attitude helps our relations with others. Feeling good about ourselves helps to build positive, healthy relationships. People enjoy working and associating with those who have an optimistic attitude. Begin today to choose positive thoughts and believe in yourself. You will be on your way to improving your self-esteem!

Attitudinal Affirmation: "I have a great attitude and work towards improving it everyday.

Belief Building Exercise: Be aware of all the positive and negative words you use in the next two days. Write them under the columns of Positive and Negative. Compare the two lists. Do your best to eliminate the negative ones from your vocabulary. Be careful not to be too "negative" with yourself when you slip.

Change Producing Action: Consciously attempt to interact with everyone with whom you come in contact today in a positive manner. Be aware of what pushes your "hot button" in order to avoid conflict and be able to choose to remain positive.

THOUGHTS & ACTION STEPS

B

"The subconscious mind is our servant and will work fervently to do what we program it to do."

CHAPTER 2

Beliefs

"Whether you think you can or think you can't, you're right."

Henry Ford

Belief in self means having faith in yourself and your abilities. It's being "sold" on yourself and is the cornerstone of success because you actually become what you believe about yourself. "The me I see is the me I'll be."

If you see yourself as a winner, you will think, talk, walk and act like a winner. In essence, you become a winner. Unfortunately, the same is true if you see yourself as a loser. You will perform in a manner that is consistent with the way you see yourself. Mahatma Ghandi said, "If I believe I cannot do something, it makes me incapable of doing it. But when I believe I can, then I acquire the ability to do it, even if I did not have the ability in the beginning."

Each of us possesses certain beliefs about self which are the result of information accumulated from others since birth. We have been told certain things about ourselves often enough that we have come to accept them as true, whether they are or not. It is important to remember that some of these beliefs may not only be inaccurate, but totally false. It is critical that we rid ourselves of faulty beliefs because they become our reality. The body manifests what the mind harbors.

Information received through the five senses is stored in our subconscious mind. Like a sponge, it soaks up everything. It is interesting to note that the mind does not make value judgments. To the subconscious mind, the information is neither good nor bad, simply information and, as such, processes it. An abundance of tainted information creates a negative belief system which invariably produces undesirable results. (Refer again to the Behavior Cycle in Chapter 1)

If someone were to enter our home while we were gone and dump a load of physical garbage on our living room floor, we would be extremely angry. Yet, we allow people to dump mental garbage on us everyday and, for the most part, we smile! Why? Because we don't realize how damaging it is. What kind of mental garbage? Complaining, gossiping, vulgarizing, and negative attitudes are just a few.

Exposure to this kind of negativism on a regular basis has a detrimental effect on our belief system by virtue of its entrance into our subconscious mind. According to Earl Nightingale, "You must be careful what you allow to enter your mind because your mind is like a garden. It will grow whatever is planted." So the next time you are in someone's company and this is what they're dishing out, don't ask for a plate — run! Avoid subjecting yourself to that kind of negative programming.

The good news is that we need not remain the way we are now. We can change our beliefs or "reprogram" ourselves with the tools of positive self-talk, visualization and affirmations.

Self-talk is what we say to ourselves, about ourselves. Our thoughts fall into this category, too, since they are simply unspoken words. As such, they permeate our subconscious mind as well.

If our self-talk is negative, we tend to be our own worst enemy because we blast ourselves with unkind thoughts or words. This condition can be reversed by intentionally saying and thinking positive things *to* ourselves, *about* ourselves. Using a soothing tone of voice when verbalizing is helpful.

Visualization or positive imaging is creating a mental picture of something or someone. You actually "see" it in your mind. Napoleon Hill said, "Whatever the mind can conceive and believe it can achieve." So see yourself the way you want to be. Your subconscious mind will receive this powerful message and act upon it.

An affirmation is a positive thought, consciously placed in the mind through repetition, to produce a desired result. It has three components: 1) first person, 2) present tense and 3) positive language. Always use "I" and the present tense when constructing an affirmation. For the subconscious mind, the past and future are nonexistent. Always use positive terms, too. For instance, you would say I am reaching the weight of 150 pounds instead of saying I want to lose ten pounds.

Using affirmations ensures that you're filling your mind with positive messages. You can also record them on audio tape and listen at your leisure. You need not consciously listen to them. As long as you can hear them, they are reaching the subconscious mind for storage and use. Record the affirmations with feeling and emotion.

After reading a few books on the subconscious mind several years ago, I decided to test this intriguing theory by conducting my own experiment. I enlisted the help of my wife for the project. Sue is a skilled bowler and has been actively bowling in a league for twenty-five years, since the age of twelve. I asked her to tell me some things she would like to achieve in bowling but, as of yet, had not. She replied that she would like to maintain an average of 165 (her average at the time was 156), consistently bowl games in excess of 200 and bowl a 600 scratch series in league play.

I developed several scripts on self-esteem and believing in self using very positive language. Then I constructed affirmations using some of the information from these scripts as well as from Sue's "wish list." Here are some of the affirmations exactly as they were used. "I like who I am and I feel good about myself." "I am successful and I am a winner in all aspects of my life." "I am an excellent bowler and I am maintaining an average of 165." "I am an excellent bowler and I am consistently bowling 200 + games." "I am an excellent bowler and I am bowling a 600 scratch series." These were followed by more general positive affirmations.

The next step was to record the information on audio tape. The scripts were recorded first followed by the affirmations. When recording affirmations, each one should be repeated three times. After all are recorded, each one is repeated an additional time substituting "you" for "I." For example: "You like who you are and you feel good about yourself." This has the effect of someone else affirming what you are saying about yourself.

Sue began listening to this tape two or three times a day. Six days later she called from the bowling alley to inform me she had just bowled a 603 scratch series, her first ever! Was she excited! Oddly enough, after several days she stopped listening to the tape. So I played it in the morning while she was sleeping in order for the information to enter her subconscious mind. Three weeks later she bowled a 608 and a 630 scratch series back to back weeks. Sue consistently bowled 200+ games during league play and ended the season with a 164 average, one pin below her target score. At one point her average reached 170.

Did the tape improve Sue's bowling skills? Absolutely not! What it did do was remove the psychological limitations she had placed on herself. She would position herself to bowl well and when the time came to roll those strikes or spares that would produce the desired score, the negative self-talk and beliefs would kick in. Things like: I'm not good enough, I don't deserve it, I don't have the ability, etc. This is self-sabotage and is very destructive! By reversing that kind of thinking, her true ability was able to surface bringing about the desired results.

For a brief moment the thought entered my mind about sneaking a few extra affirmations in on the tape. Things like, "I bring coffee to Curt in bed every morning" and "I cook wonderful six course meals every night." But I decided against it. Why fool around with success or get myself into trouble? Better safe than sorry. Margaret didn't raise a fool!

Remember, the subconscious mind is our servant and will work fervently to do what we program it to do. Faithfully using the powerful tools of positive self-talk, visualization and affirmations will provide the subconscious mind with verbal and visual instruction on the kind of person you want to become. It will work unceasingly to make it become a reality. That is its nature. Our subconscious mind can be our best friend or worst enemy, depending upon the script we give it. By itself, it is neutral.

Believe only the best about yourself. Believe that you are good, kind, capable, loving and successful and you will notice a marked difference in how you see yourself. This will result in greater achievement and higher self-esteem. Believe the best about yourself!

Attitudinal Affirmation: "I am a kind, generous, successful person."

Belief Building Exercise: Make a list of what you believe about yourself. Decide if these beliefs work for you or not. Forget about those that are holding you back or causing problems. Concentrate on the ones that build your esteem and promote success.

Change Producing Action: Share with a close friend all the things you believe about yourself and your plans to focus on your positive qualities. Make a commitment to follow through and ask your friend to keep you on task.

"The me I see is the me I'll be!"

C

"We are born with only two fears, the fear of falling and the fear of loud noises. All the rest of our fears are learned."

CHAPTER 3

Confidence

"Our doubts are traitors, and make us lose the good we oft might win, by fearing to attempt."[1]

William Shakespeare

Self-confidence is the assurance of one's ability or feeling sure of oneself. Confidence is developed by taking positive risks, attempting a task with no guarantee of success and having the distinct possibility of failure. Start with small tasks in order to experience success, and use them as stepping-stones or building blocks to more challenging ones. Success breeds success. There is nothing like it for building confidence.

You can't steal second base with one foot clinging to first. One of three things can happen in an attempted steal. You might get picked off at first. You may get thrown out at second. Or you might be successful in your effort to steal the base. But you will never know until you step off the bag and take the risk. The same is true in life. Playing it safe gets you nowhere.

It takes courage to take a risk. Contrary to what many people believe, courage is not the absence of fear. No! Courage is being afraid to do something but doing it in spite of your fear. Cus D'Amato, a famous boxing trainer, said "Heroes and cowards are acted upon by the same fear. They just respond differently." The hero advances while the coward retreats.

We are born with only two fears, the fear of falling and the fear of loud noises. All the rest of our fears are learned and, through repetition, are driven deep into our subconscious mind where they begin to dictate, dominate and control our beliefs and ultimately, our actions. Our fears take over and prevent us from taking risks. What are some of these fears? The fear of failure, success, ridicule and criticism from the horn honkers. Who are the horn honkers? This story illustrates.

A lady was driving down Canal Street in New Orleans. She stopped at a red traffic light, and as she did her car engine died. She tried in vain to start it. Her second attempt failed as well. By this time the traffic light turned green. The man in the car behind her honked his horn. Another effort on her part proved just as futile as before. Honk, honk, honk came the sound from the car behind her. Now she had flooded the engine and would be going nowhere. The impatient man behind her just sat on his horn — Hoooooonnnnnnnnk! The lady very calmly stepped out of her car, walked to the rear and said to the driver, "Excuse me, sir. If you would be so kind as to try to start my car for me, I'd be more than happy to sit here and honk your horn for you!"

The world is full of horn honkers. They are the spectators of life who sit in the stands or on the sidelines and complain, criticize and condemn but never, ever are a part of the game themselves — because they lack the courage! So why worry about them? Go ahead and take a risk! Ann-Margaret's character, Ariel, in the movie "Grumpy Old Men", said, "The thing you'll regret most about life is the risks you weren't willing to take." I'm talking about risks as a means of growth, not life challenging ones. For instance, I took a big risk just last week. I tried to learn how to program my VCR!

Fear causes us to want to stay in our comfort zone. That's the place in our mind where we feel safe, that is nonthreatening and where we know what to expect. Our comfort zone does not remain the same. It becomes larger or smaller depending upon our willingness to risk. It can be as small as a postage stamp or as large as the world relative to our level of confidence. Staying in our comfort zone causes us to become stagnant.

I have learned that the best way to overcome fear is to face it. As a young boy in elementary school, I was deathly afraid to speak in front of a group. I was so shy I couldn't lead the group in silent prayer. Yet, I was elected president of the 4-H Club in fifth and sixth grade. I dreaded the meetings. With my heart racing a mile a minute, hands clammy and voice quivering, I reluctantly stood before the club members and conducted the meeting. I hated every minute of it and was glad when it was over. That experience caused me to avoid those kinds of situations for a long time.

I successfully avoided getting in front of groups until my junior year in college. I postponed taking the dreaded speech course as long as I could, but it was inevitable. I struggled through it and managed to survive, but I still didn't like it. Not only did I feel the trauma as I was giving the speech, but many hours prior to it as well. I was miserable.

As I began my teaching career, I was never nervous in front of the students. Yet, with the faculty, fear took charge. Knowing I wanted to make a point at a faculty meeting, the same physical maladies from the 4-H experience would haunt me. It was still difficult for me as an adult, but I knew at some point I must face it.

I began to volunteer for tasks that required me to get in front of a group. This involved leadership positions in civic and professional organizations, making presentations to other school faculties, and serving as a lector in my church. The more I did it, the less nervous I became. Finally, one day I noticed I was not only not nervous, I was actually enjoying it! Imagine that! What a change! Only because I faced my fear and would not allow it to defeat me was I able to overcome it.

The irony is that today I am a professional speaker. Do I still have butterflies before a speaking engagement? Occasionally. As a speaker, the key is not to get rid of the butterflies but to have them fly in formation!

A ship is safe in a harbor, but that is not the purpose for which it was built. We, like the ship, must leave port and travel unknown waters. We must take the risk. That's how we grow and develop self-confidence and at the same time, build our self-esteem.

Attitudinal Affirmation: "I have confidence in myself and I take positive risks."

Belief Building Exercise: Recall the times you had the opportunity to take a risk in the last year and did not. List them on a sheet of paper and next to each one, put the reason you failed to try.

Change Producing Action: Carefully examine those opportunities. Select one and make the commitment to actively pursue it and follow through. Go for it!

THOUGHTS & ACTION STEPS

D

"In reality, by making no decision, they have actually made one. "

CHAPTER 4

Decision-Making

"There is no more miserable human being than the one in whom nothing is habitual but indecision."

William James

Decision-making is a part of everyday life — at home, in school and on the job. It is a fact of life. It means making up our minds and making choices, things we must confront each day. For some, nothing could be worse than making a decision. Often times this is true of people with low self-esteem. They don't believe in themselves nor have sufficient confidence to be convinced that they can make the right choice. As someone once said, "I used to be indecisive, but now I'm not so sure."

Opportunities abound for making decisions every day. Many of them are small and inconsequential; however, some are serious and should not be taken lightly. What we wear, where we eat or what movie we attend will not affect world peace. But buying a new house or car, changing jobs or selecting a mate carry with them significant consequences and require serious thought and consideration.

Some people agonize over making any kind of decision. Fearful of making the wrong one, they make none at all hoping the situation resolves itself or simply disappears. In reality, by making no decision, they have actually made one. They have decided not to decide and, in my opinion, that is worse than making the wrong one or none at all. This is called living by default.

As the indecision continues, their self-esteem takes a beating and decision-making becomes even more difficult. It is a self-fulfilling prophecy and can only be broken by having the courage to make a decision, even if the outcome is less than satisfactory. It's like the old saying, "Bad breath is better than no breath at all!"

One thing is certain, though. Who we are and what we are today are the result of all the decisions we have made in our lifetime. We are a product of our choices and will continue to be until we leave this earth. Learning to make the right choices and decisions will enhance our self-esteem and improve the quality of our life.

There is no one best method for making decisions. Use what works best for you. That makes sense! However, I will offer a plan in the event you do not have one. It is simple, to the point and easy to use.

The first step is to pick a decision you must make. Start with something that's not too difficult or complicated. State the situation and the decision to be made. Write it out so that you can see it clearly. Brainstorm to determine all possible choices or alternatives. Now list all the possibilities. Using two columns, list the positive and negative consequences for each alternative. Use this information to conclude which alternative will produce your desired outcome.

Rank your choices and try your favorite one first. Evaluate the results. If you are not satisfied, go back to the previous step and work with your second choice. Continue this process until you feel like you are on target. If none are acceptable, you can brainstorm for more alternatives or simply choose the one that is most palatable to you.

Do not second guess yourself! If you do, you are setting yourself up for failure by sabotaging your confidence in your ability to make a decision. If the decision produces less than satisfactory results, carefully scrutinize the possibilities and proceed to your next choice. You erred and that's O.K. It only shows your humanity. Remember, hindsight is 20-20, foresight isn't as good. Continually working with this process will help you to become a better decision-maker.

Not all decisions are based on logic and reason. Sometimes you need to follow your heart. One of the most crucial decisions I have made in my life was to leave the education profession to pursue a career in professional speaking. After twenty-four successful years as a teacher and administrator and the distinct possibility of more promotions, I knew there were other things I wanted to do with my life. Through much prayer, Sue and I jointly made the decision for me to leave the security of the educational system in order to pursue my dream. It was purely a spiritual decision, no logic or reason involved.

When following your heart, project yourself into the perceived situation and notice how your body feels. If you sense peace and excitement as opposed to restlessness and flatness, you're probably on the right track. Listen to your body, especially your heart and gut.

One danger we face after making a decision is that we don't give it enough time to play out or develop. We are impatient and want instant results. And when it doesn't happen, we're ready to try something else or repeat what we were doing before.

I fell into this trap. I thought I would make a lateral move from education to speaking and experience immediate success. This was not the case. I was back to square one in speaking and wasn't satisfied with it. But that was the reality of it. Persistence and determination over the years have allowed me to progress steadily in my new field. I needed to pay my dues here, too, just as in education! I witness to this in order to remind you that it often takes time to see the fruits of your decision, to know whether or not adjustments are needed.

Learn to face life's challenges and become a confident decision-maker. You will be glad you did and will feel good about yourself, too.

Attitudinal Affirmation: "I have the confidence necessary to make good decisions every day."

Belief Building Exercise: Call to mind all the decisions pending in your life at the moment. Write them on a sheet of paper. Prioritize and select the one most pressing.

Change Producing Action: Commit to addressing your pressing decision immediately. Use the process described in this chapter to help you reach a decision. Share this commitment with your spouse or a close friend.

THOUGHTS & ACTION STEPS

E

"Enthusiasm is a necessary ingredient for success."

CHAPTER 5

Enthusiasm

"Without enthusiasm there is no progress in the world."

Woodrow Wilson

The word enthusiasm comes from two Greek words, "en" and "theos" meaning "in God" and "to have God within." In reality, enthusiasm is already within us by virtue of God's spirit. The key is to let it flow out of us everyday. To be enthusiastic is to be very interested in something or excited about it. In a sense it is being high spirited.

We should approach every day with enthusiasm, for nothing great was ever achieved without it. Whatever your task or job today, be grateful for it. Tackle it with vim and vigor, as though it were the most important chore in the world and you will do it better. Enthusiasm is an inner fire that fuels the furnace of achievement.

It matters not whether you are a brain surgeon or garbage collector, enthusiasm will enable you to do a better job. Imagine waiting for surgery in the operating room and the doctor looks down at you and says, "Gee whiz, I'm really not in the mood to do this today! I'm just not into it!" What would you do? How would you feel? You know the answer as well as I. You would jump off of that gurney and literally run for your life. And who would blame you?

Enthusiasm is a necessary ingredient for success. It's the powerful engine that drives us and provides the motivation to face life and all of its challenges. It also helps in finding solutions to those challenges. We become excited about life and living as we learn to make the most of each day.

A button was given to me by a friend which says, "Enjoy life. This is not a dress rehearsal!" So true! We may as well enjoy ourselves because we are not going to get out of this life alive. So go for the gusto! A billboard outside of a church read, "If you're tired of sin, come in." And below it someone wrote, "If you're not, call 375-7326!" Now that's enthusiasm!

Some people drag themselves out of bed each morning wishing they could sleep until noon. They get up, go through the motions at work, then come home and walk around in a daze until it's time to go to bed again. They're already dreading getting up the next morning. What a life! No excitement, no enthusiasm, no living! These are the kind of people who can brighten up a room — just by leaving it! I know some folks like that and you do, too. Don't allow yourself to be one of them.

You need to wake up each morning as though it were going to be your last day on earth — and one day you are going to be right. I tell Sue often that I'm going to live to be one hundred. Her response is, "You would do that to me, wouldn't you?" What a kidder! I tell Sue this and believe it but there are no guarantees. I don't have a contract with God for a certain number of years on this earth.

And because of this, I try to live each day to the fullest and with enthusiasm. Somehow the word "terminal" takes on a new meaning at an airport when I fly U.S. Air. Seeing that sign reminds me to go for it. I've come to realize that too many people are interested in life after death and not concerned enough about life after birth.

I use the telephone as a means of conveying enthusiasm. Some might say that a telephone in my hands could be considered a lethal weapon. Nonetheless, I have fun with it. It began several years ago with the message on my answering machine. I recorded the usual message but ended with a positive thought, such as, "Life is like a piano — what you get out of it depends on how you play it." Every week or so I recorded a new ending.

Several months later I changed the ending to "Make yourself a great day!" Sue said, "Curt, that doesn't make sense." "Of course it does," I replied. "The message I am trying to send is that your day will be exactly what you make of it. You're the architect of your day and design it according to your own specifications."

Then I really became creative. I decided to take all of the elements of the recorded message and put them together in the form of a rap song. So if you call my home now this is what you will hear on the answering machine:

Yo! You've reached the motivation man and my name is Curt
You know I'll call you back soon cause I'm always alert.
Leave your name and your number when you hear the beep
And stay close to your phone cause I never really sleep!

I believe in commitment so I'll call back in a hurry
Let the motivation man take away all your worry.
So relax and be cool and leave your message in a plan
Cause you're in good hands with the motivation man!

Sue's comment was, "Who in the world is going to hire you after listening to something like that?" I said, " I don't know, but at least they'll know I have a sense of humor and am enthusiastic about what I do." The response has been very positive to the "song", but one caller told me not to quit my day job. He was joking, I think.

I have actually had people call hoping to reach the machine to hear the message and expressed disappointment in hearing me "live." So I put the machine on and tell them to dial again. Every time I consider changing the message, someone invariably gives me great feedback and I don't have the heart to do it. Since nothing remains the same, I am sure it will eventually change. But for the moment, yo!

Sometime during last year, the country singers Wynona Judd and Clint Black were featured on the cover of TV Guide magazine. Wynona's quote beneath the picture was, "Life's too short to work with ugly men!" Now there's enthusiasm! And as I look around, some of us are lucky to be employed at all!

Regardless of where you live or what you do, it's important for you to associate with enthusiastic people. If you don't, those around you will bring you down with them into a rut. And the only difference between a rut and a grave is some three feet.

Enthusiasm is contagious. Be a carrier and spread it to everyone! They will be glad you did and so will you. You'll begin to see yourself as an exciting, vibrant person enjoying life to the fullest.

Attitudinal Affirmation: "I wake up each morning filled with energy and enthusiasm."

Belief Building Exercise: Determine all of the tasks you must perform today. List them on a sheet of paper.

Change Producing Action: Pick the task you least enjoy doing from your list. Commit to approaching it with enthusiasm and joy. Do this daily until it becomes a habit.

F

"Building faith in ourselves is very similar to eating a shrimp poboy sandwich, we do it one bite at a time."

CHAPTER 6

Faith

> *"I assure you, if you had faith the size of a mustard seed, you would be able to say to this mountain, 'Move from here to there,' and it would move. Nothing would be impossible for you."*
>
> Matthew 17:20

Faith is trust and believing without having proof. When we have faith, we believe without seeing which is totally contrary to the adage, "Seeing is believing." It is a quality that does not come naturally; it must be developed and nurtured. It is advanced incrementally over a period of time.

Persons with low self-esteem have little or no faith in themselves. They put themselves down and are reluctant to attempt a task because they believe failure is imminent. This is the beginning of a lifetime of missed opportunities, low achievement and a willingness to settle for less than they deserve. They resolve themselves to the fact that this is the way it is and accept it.

In discussing faith, I would like to focus on three aspects: faith in God, faith in self and faith in others. All are substantial in developing and maintaining high self-esteem.

Trusting in God is true faith, for that is believing without seeing. Faith in God is developed once we have established a relationship with Him. This is done through prayer and by getting to know Him. It can be difficult at times because our prayers are not always answered the way we want. Only the person with unwavering faith can accept this as God's will and move on. Again, not an easy thing to do!

It has been said that we must have the faith of a little child. Children tend to be very trusting because, for the most part, they have not yet experienced disappointment and hurt from adults. They also believe that God will answer their prayers and meet all of their needs. They put their whole heart and soul in that belief.

At the age of three, my niece, Sera, was diagnosed with Acute Lymphocytic Leukemia and was admitted to Children's Hospital in New Orleans. Sue was distraught and crying as she visited her one day. Sera looked up at Sue and said, "Don't worry nanny, God hasn't finished healing me yet." A nurse present at the time asked, "What did she say?" Sera repeated, "I said that God hasn't finished healing me yet." From the mouths of babes, a three year old!

Three days later she went into total remission. It was a long, slow, difficult recovery. But today, ten years later at the age of thirteen, Sera is a beautiful, healthy adolescent attending middle school. This is complete trust and faith in God for which we, as adults, should strive. When seeking faith, we need to make an effort to be childlike and more trusting.

My faith in God has wavered at times in recent years when discouragement set in. But as I write this chapter today, Good Friday, I recommit myself to be more trusting in God and His will for me.

We must also develop faith in ourselves. This is very closely related to belief in ourselves which was discussed in

Chapter 2; therefore, I will not belabor the point. Each one of us, though, has certain innate abilities given to us by God. A lack of faith in ourselves prevents us from developing and using these assets. In essence, they are wasted. Printed on my business card is Phillipians 4:13, "I can do all things through Christ who strengthens me." This reminds me that I am capable of doing many things but only through the grace and strength of God.

A lack of faith causes us to believe that others can do an assignment better than we can. We are afraid we might embarrass ourselves so we stay in the background, refuse to volunteer and allow our self-esteem to erode. This is so self-defeating.

The most effective way to build faith in ourselves is to believe that we can do a task; then step forward and take the risk. The risk should be small enough at first so that if it does not succeed, the result will not be devastating to our self-esteem. Consider it a learning experience. Analyze what went wrong and transfer this new information to your next task. Learn from your mistakes and avoid repeating them. One definition of insanity is to keep doing the same things repeatedly expecting different results. Rather than opting for insanity, simply make the necessary adjustments.

On the other hand, completing a task successfully is the beginning of a foundation from which we gain confidence. Building faith in ourselves is very similar to eating a shrimp poboy sandwich, we do it one bite at a time. That way it becomes more manageable and less overwhelming.

Having faith in others requires dependability. By keeping their word and living up to their commitments, trust is instilled. Little time is wasted determining whom we can put our faith in and whom we cannot. We discover very quickly who can be trusted. Mutual faith and trust must stand the test of time. It is only after repeatedly doing what we say we will do that we feel confident with each other.

Faith is a must in all relationships, whether they be family, friends, spouse or business. Any breech of faith causes serious problems and sometimes even destroys the relationship. No friendship or working relationship can exist on suspicion, mistrust and broken promises.

Faith is to believe what we do not see, and the reward for this faith is to see what we believe. Faith in God, in ourselves and in others provides the strength to see ourselves and others in a positive manner. When we do this, we enhance our self-esteem and position ourselves for healthy relationships.

Attitudinal Affirmation: "I have unwavering faith in myself and others."

Belief Building Exercise: Make a list of the people in whom you have faith. Consider yourself, too. Write the reason(s) next to each one why you do have faith in them.

Change Producing Action: Contact several of the people on your list and let them know that you have faith in them. Tell them why. A suggestion would be to send it in a letter so they can keep it as a memento. You will boost their self-esteem as well as strengthen the relationship.

THOUGHTS & ACTION STEPS

G

"Goals are simply dreams with a deadline."

CHAPTER 7

GOALS

"I believe this nation should commit itself to achieving the goal of putting a man on the moon before this decade is out."

JOHN F. KENNEDY

A goal is something we want to accomplish or achieve. It is what we want to be, where we want to go, what we want to do, or what we want to have. Goals provide purpose and direction to our lives.

A stranger was driving in the country one day and came to a fork in the road. Not knowing which way to go, he asked an old farmer who was sitting on a tree stump, "Where will these roads take me?" The farmer asked, "Where do you want to go?" "I really don't know," replied the stranger. "Then either road will get you there," said the farmer. If we do not know where we want to go in life, then it does not matter what road we travel. To get somewhere you must know where you are going. As Yogi Berra, the great baseball player, once said, "If you don't know where you are going, you might end up someplace else." He is also credited with saying, "When you come to a fork in the road, take it!"

Goals provide a blueprint for our lives. Would we hire a carpenter and tell him to build a house for us? Whatever he wants? That any kind of house will do? Of course not! There is no way we would allow him to make that decision. We would provide a blueprint from an architect and instruct him to follow the plans exactly. And he had better not deviate from it one fraction or we would fire him! Yet, many people are willing to go through life with no master blueprint, floundering around from day to day allowing other people to "build" their lives for them, to live their lives for them.

Most people don't plan to fail, they simply fail to plan. Oddly enough, many people spend more time deciding what television programs to watch, preparing for a golf match or planning a New Year's Eve party than they do charting their life's course.

Goals also help to harness, focus and concentrate our energy and effort. Go outside on a bright, sunny day with the sun at your back, a sheet of paper in one hand and a magnifying glass in the other. Now move the magnifying glass over the sheet of paper. What happens? Nothing. Why? Because you have not held the magnifying glass in one spot long enough to concentrate the sun's energy.

Now take the same three elements: the sun, a sheet of paper and the magnifying glass and hold the glass very still over the paper. What happens now? A hole is burned and the paper catches fire. Goals do the same thing for us.

Goals are simply dreams with a deadline. Speaking of dreams, I had one as a middle school principal. My dream was that all middle school students would reach puberty on the same day — and we would have no school that day! As you might suspect it never happened, but it was a great dream!

Dreams get you going but goals keep you on course. In order to help you get on the right track, I am going to suggest a simple plan for setting goals. You may have seen variations of it elsewhere, but I know this one works. I have used it successfully for several years.

The first step is to decide what you want to accomplish or achieve. Clearly identify your goal. Two men were hiking in the woods. Looking ahead, they spotted a huge grizzly bear charging toward them. One of the men immediately sat down and began taking off his hiking boots and putting on his running shoes. His partner asked him, "What do you think you are doing? You can't outrun that bear." The other hiker looked up at him and said, "I don't have to outrun that bear. I just have to outrun you!" He clearly identified his goal and so must you.

The next step is to state your goal in positive terms. For example, instead of saying I want to lose ten pounds, say I will reach the weight of 130. Always work with the positive and avoid the negative. Now put your goal in writing and post it where you will see it everyday. Writing it out provides the subconscious mind with a clear direction of what you want to pursue and seeing it daily provides regular reinforcement.

Now you need to set a target date for completion. Doing this indicates you have made a commitment to follow through. Without it, you will probably procrastinate and lose sight of your goal. As a principal, my summer schedule was very flexible. I remember one summer sitting in the recliner in early June preparing my list of "honey do" jobs for the months ahead. Sue asked what I was doing. I said, "I'm making a list of all the things I have to do around the house this summer." She looked at me and said, "Well, why don't you use the list you made last year. You didn't do any of them!" I really didn't like hearing that, but she was right. I had good intentions in June, but without a completion date I lacked commitment. August was there and I was back in school full-time. The list was ambitious, but it wasn't done and proved useless.

The next step is to develop an action plan. This is really the nuts and bolts of the goal-setting process. Here is where you lay out what you must do to accomplish your goal. It is necessary to determine the following: what you must do, what information or knowledge you must have, what skills are needed, who can help you, what obstacles you must overcome, etc. Having a goal without a plan is just a wish, and wishing never made anything happen.

Imagine the football coach walking into the faculty lounge and someone asking him what the team will do Friday night and he says, "We're going to win." Then he is asked how. He responds, "Well, we're going to show up, do the best we can and win the game!" Who would buy that? Rest assured, he has a plan. He has scouted the opposition and knows their strengths and weaknesses and developed a plan accordingly. We, too, must go into life with a strong game plan.

The next step is to read and review your goals daily. This not only drives them into your subconscious mind, but also serves as a constant reminder of what you are striving to do. It helps to keep you focused.

Now visualize your goals. See yourself as already having achieved them. Again, you are programming the subconscious which will help you to be successful. If you have trouble visualizing your goals, I suspect it is because you don't really believe you're capable of achieving them. Concentrate hard and see them in your mind.

Evaluate your progress periodically to determine how you are doing. Make any adjustments necessary. Your target date was not set in stone. It was merely an arbitrary timeline you established to keep on course. If you need more time, take it! If you finish early, great! You may have to change some steps in your action plan because of unforeseen circumstances. That's O.K., too. What is most important is to keep progressing and never give up.

And last, celebrate when you accomplish your goal! Be good to yourself! You set out to do something and you did it. Be proud! But don't stop there. While you are on a high, set more goals and continue the process!

This plan is easy to implement, so adopt it! But several things are important to remember when setting goals. First, they must be attainable or you will be setting yourself up for failure. Second, they should be just out of reach, but not out of sight. Your goals should make you stretch in order for you to grow. And last, there should be balance. Set goals in all areas of your life. Don't try to catch all your crawfish with only one net if you want to be successful.

Consider setting family, personal, career, physical, spiritual and/or social goals. I have done this for years, and it has proven very helpful. For example, one of my physical goals has been to keep my weight at or below 155 pounds. After my illness as a teenager, my weight gradually increased until it reached a high of 185 pounds by the end of my first year of teaching. Now, I'm the first to admit that 185 pounds is not enough weight to qualify going hunting bears with a switch, but on a guy who stands 5'7", it's more than enough to make me look pleasantly plump.

I did not like myself at that weight, so I lost thirty pounds in 1965 and have kept it off. One of my friends recently told me I was lucky that I didn't have a weight problem. I asked what did he mean. He said, "I've known you all these years and your weight has remained the same." I replied, "While I'm jogging two miles and walking three several times a week in ninety-five degree heat and ninety percent humidity and you're sitting in your air conditioned living room eating a bowl of Breyers ice cream, you call *me* lucky!" Luck has nothing to do with it. It is a personal, conscious choice I make and achieve by setting a goal. I must exercise because I have a physical problem — my body retains ice cream!

It hasn't been easy maintaining my weight over the years because I enjoy sweets. As a kid I dreamed of being 6'4", weighing 110 pounds and living next door to a bakery. Obviously, that did not happen. But through a combination of exercise and diet (sweets) outlined in my action plan, I have been successful in keeping my weight constant. Not an easy task, but one that can be accomplished with a goal and a little self-discipline.

Setting goals keeps us and everyone around us on task. It is like the cross-eyed javelin thrower — he doesn't set many records but he keeps the crowd alert. Goalsetters are achievers! As you reach your goals, you will raise your self-esteem, too.

Attitudinal Affirmation: "I am setting and achieving worthwhile goals now."

Belief Building Exercise: Think of all the things you would like to accomplish in your life. Examine all the possibilities. Put them in writing.

Change Producing Action: Select one goal from the list above and develop a detailed plan using the steps mentioned in the chapter. Stick with it through completion and write me concerning your success. I look forward to hearing from you.

THOUGHTS & ACTION STEPS

H

"With honesty, it is all or none. You are either honest or you are not."

CHAPTER 8

HONESTY

"If you tell the truth, you don't have to remember anything."
MARK TWAIN

Most of us grew up with our parents or family members telling us that "honesty is the best policy." I don't know if it is the best, but no doubt it is an effective one. An honest person does not lie, cheat or steal. These are important qualities when looking for friends, employment and people with whom we do business. We want to be treated fairly and feel comfortable with those around us.

But honesty, like many other things, begins with us. We tell the truth not so much to be believed, but to believe ourselves. So if we expect others to be honest, we must be honest with them, too. I dare say if I were to ask if you are an honest person your reply would be a resounding "yes!" You might even be insulted that I asked.

The truth of the matter is that many of us are honest in big issues but tend to fudge somewhat in the small ones. For instance. Have you been completely honest in filling out a job application, a bank loan, your income tax forms or papers for insurance coverage? Do you obey the speed limit? Have you ever run a red light? Do you come to a complete stop at a "stop" sign? I believe it is safe to say that most of us cut corners, figuratively and literally, from time to time. And when we do, we feel as guilty as a cat with canary breath. But relax,

I'm not pointing a finger, just providing food for thought.

In performing our daily actions, we would do well to follow the advice of Thomas Jefferson. "Whenever you are to do a thing, though it can never be known but to yourself, ask yourself how you would act were all the world looking at you, and act accordingly." It is a good guide to follow. Doing the right thing allows you to feel good about yourself because you had the opportunity to do wrong, and did not.

Lessons are to be learned in athletics as well. Golf has been described "as a game where when you don't succeed, you try, try and try again. And if you are honest, you mark it down on the scorecard." Believe me, I've been there. Golf may be the only professional sport where participants are not hovered over by an official or referee. Much of the time while on the course the players are on the honor system.

Tom Kite is an outstanding professional golfer who played collegiately at the University of Texas. In a major tournament a few years ago, his golf ball inadvertently moved while he was attempting to remove small pieces of debris near it. Any movement of the ball without being struck with a club is a violation of the rules and calls for a one stroke penalty. No one saw his ball move but him, yet without hesitation, Kite notified the nearest official and assessed himself the penalty stroke.

Sports enthusiasts and television commentators were making a big deal over his actions. Kite calmly replied, "I don't know what all the fuss is about. That's the rules and we play by them if the game is going to maintain its integrity."

Can we all learn a lesson from this? Think of the kind of world we could have if everyone played by the rules of life. Without question it would be a much better place to live and raise our children. Someone once advised, "Lead your life in such a way that you wouldn't be ashamed to sell the family parrot to the town gossip." That is good advice. There would be total honesty and absolutely nothing to hide.

Instead, we routinely learn from the news media of elected government officials being indicted for wrongdoing. They violate public trust apparently believing their dishonesty will not be discovered. One week they are on the cover of TIME, and the next week they are doing it.

This is an indictment of our society, but I am convinced things are improving. People appear to be more careful who they vote for and then for holding those elected accountable. A father was reading a bedtime story to his five year old daughter. She looked up at him and asked, "Daddy, do all fairy tales begin with 'once upon a time?'" "Oh, no, sweetheart," he answered. "Many of them begin with 'if I'm elected!'"

Fairy tale or not, we should not expect honesty only from public officials. It must be prevalent in our home, school, worksite and community, too. It ought to begin in the home, then filter into the other areas. The lyrics, "let there be peace on earth and let it begin with me" are appropriate for honesty as well. It could just as easily be sung, "Let there be honesty in the world and let it begin with me." That's the best place to start. What a tremendous difference it would make if everyone adopted this approach. Honesty should be the guiding principle in everything we do.

We come in contact with people everyday and assume they are honest unless given a reason to believe otherwise. A few years ago I was flying from Pennsylvania to Illinois. As we began the descent into Chicago, I looked out of the window and noticed another airplane very close to us. We appeared to be heading for the same runway. I was a little bit more than concerned about this, so I alerted the guy sitting next to me. Seeing his eyes enlarge, I assumed we were in deep trouble. A lot of chattering and buzzing began and the topic of conversation wasn't the mystery meal we had for dinner. They saw the other plane, too!

In an attempt to avoid panic, the flight attendant made an announcement on the intercom. She said, "Folks, if you'll look out the right side of the aircraft, you'll see another aircraft." Now there was a news flash! She continued, "But don't worry. O'Hare Airport provides for simultaneous landings on parallel runways." Say what? She repeated the announcement. The two planes were really close by this time. So I told the person next to me, "Look, if she'd lie to us about those peanuts being fresh, she'd lie to us about that other airplane, too! Let's keep a close eye on it." As though that would achieve anything. However, sometimes we have no choice. We must take at face value what someone tells us and hope they're being honest.

With honesty, it is all or none. You are either honest or you are not. Take care to be totally honest in all your interactions with people. They will avoid you if you are not. Here is more food for thought: How is it we trust banks with our money but they don't trust us with their pens? (They are attached to those little chains) It might be a good question for your banker. Perhaps he knows something we don't. Regardless, be honest in all your dealings and you will be proud of the person you see. Honest you will!

Attitudinal Affirmation: "I am an honest person."

Belief Building Exercise: Reflect on the last twelve months and recognize the times you fudged on the truth.

Change Producing Action: Pick several of these occurrences and determine to perform them in a way that will make you proud.

I

"In essence, what we become is directly linked to our ability to imagine."

CHAPTER 9

IMAGINATION

"The man who has no imagination has no wings."
MUHAMMED ALI

Imagination is the power of forming pictures in the mind of things not present to the senses. It is also the ability to create new things or ideas, or to combine old ones in new forms. It is the working tool of the creative person. Poets, inventors and artists would be stymied without it. But so would we.

According to Psychologist Carl Young, "Imagination is the concentrated extract of all forces of life and our future lives are limited only by the tether of our imaginations." In essence, what we become is directly linked to our ability to imagine. Our future is shaped, in part, by our imagination.

As youngsters, imagination was our magic carpet taking us to far off places or allowing us to become someone we admired. It was quite normal to be piloting a spaceship in another galaxy or throwing the winning touchdown in the waning seconds of a football game. Imagination allowed us to transcend time and space.

As we grew older, our ability to use our imagination slowly faded away. Whether or not it was because we thought mature people did not fantasize or those around us told us to get into the real world is hard to determine. I suspect it was probably a combination of the two. Nevertheless, the "use it or lose it" principle prevailed and most of us lost it.

That may be why so few people have dreams today. Without an active imagination, they can not see themselves beyond where they are now. Or if they can, they are embarrassed or unwilling to admit it. They trudge along thinking that life has no more to offer them than this.

A philosopher once wrote, "There's not much to do but bury a man when the last of his dreams is dead." At this point he is just existing, going through the motions like a zombie. Technically, he is dead. He just hasn't been buried yet. What a terrible way to live! It reminds me of a cartoon showing a picture of a tombstone. The inscription read, "Here lies Jane Smith, died at thirty-four, buried at sixty-two." Unfortunately, there are too many Jane Smiths in the world today.

Dreams allow us to see ourselves as we can be, not necessarily as we are. That does not mean we are not good the way we are. It simply means we can be better. Working towards our dreams gives us a good reason to get out of bed every morning. My dream is to speak all over the world and to write books. I have not achieved it yet, but I am working on it and making progress. You are reading part of that dream right now. I believe Eleanor Roosevelt was right in saying, "The future belongs to those who believe in their dreams."

Imagination can be used in both positive and negative ways. It is within your power to choose, so be careful. In addition to dreams, imagination has been a key factor in the invention or development of everything we have today. Every item you can think of had its beginning in someone's imagination. The airplane, automobile, computer, radio and telephone all began as a figment of someone's imagination. Can you imagine our world without them?

Another positive use of the imagination is in our work. Think of the boredom of doing the same thing repeatedly the same way. Without imagination, everything would become dull and routine, eventually leading to mediocrity. Finding new and creative ways of getting the job done keeps us interested, motivated and more productive. It will do a lot for our sanity, too. When patterns are broken, new worlds emerge.

Limitations and boundaries are removed when we turn our imagination loose. That is what happens when we use the brainstorming technique. Ideas and possibilities surface that would not have been thought of had logic been used. It unleashes the thought process and gives the brain freedom to roam.

The most common negative use of imagination is worry. Worry is the misuse of the imagination. We allow all kinds of scenarios to form in our minds that are detrimental to our physical and emotional well-being. Dr. Charles Mayo said, "Worry affects the circulation, the heart, the glands, the whole nervous system and profoundly affects the health."

Also, a noted psychologist stated that worry is the personality's most disintegrating enemy. Worrying is like rocking in a rocking chair, it gives you something to do but it doesn't get you anywhere. About ninety percent of what people worry about never happens. Today is the tomorrow you worried about yesterday, and all is well. This is powerful stuff and should convince you to stop worrying.

People sometimes use their imagination in ingenious ways. Said one dad, "On long trips, I like to play games with my kids when they get too rambunctious. My personal favorite is called, 'What would you do if dad dropped you off here?'" That will draw their attention and perhaps cause them to use their imagination at the same time.

Use your imagination often. Imagine yourself doing the kind of things that help you feel good about yourself. It's your most creative tool. Your imagination leaps ahead to the places you have yet to see. You are in the cockpit and you are the pilot. So take off and let your imagination fly!

Attitudinal Affirmation: "I use my imagination in new and creative ways."

Belief Building Exercise: Determine when you have used your imagination in the last month. Record whether these times were positive or negative experiences.

Change Producing Action: Select something you would like to do but have not done. For the next week consciously imagine yourself doing it. Now do it!

THOUGHTS & ACTION STEPS

J

"Joy is an internal job."

CHAPTER 10

Joy

"One joy dispels a hundred cares."

Oriental Proverb

Joy is to experience pleasure or delight. It is an intimate feeling and a state of happiness. Like so many other things in life, it is a choice. Joy is an internal "job." Our life is either a celebration or a chore. It depends upon us. We are all blessed with unique gifts and given a special purpose in life by God. Joy is His way of letting us know if we are on track with our purpose, or, as I often say, "on purpose."

In the race to be better or best, don't miss the joy of being. Enjoy the moment, for that is all we have. Learn not only to stop and smell the roses, but to enjoy them as well. (I don't mind stopping to smell the roses as long as I don't have to keep up the flower bed!) There is nothing wrong with wanting more in life as long as we appreciate and value what we already have. Discontent is the price we pay for not being grateful for what we have. We end up throwing "pity parties" for ourselves because tunnel vision has caused us to lose sight of how fortunate we really are.

We tend to take so much for granted everyday instead of counting our blessings. Sue and I had gone to a movie in New Orleans and stopped at a fast food restaurant for a quick meal. As I was standing in line, a young lady entered the building. She had no arms. I didn't know how to react at first, so I just stood there waiting for my order. She placed her order and maneuvered the purse between her neck and shoulder. The cashier took the proper amount of money and returned the purse to her.

As I looked into her eyes, I expected to see frustration and anger. But to my surprise, all I saw was peace and joy. She managed to put the bag of food between her neck and shoulders with her purse and began walking toward the door. I moved in that direction to assist her, but she simply backed into the door, opened it, smiled and walked out.

I was deeply moved by this experience. How difficult it must be to live life with such a handicap, yet she seemed perfectly content and dealt with it so admirably. I felt ashamed of the many times I had griped and complained about petty annoyances and inconveniences in my life. I realized that I needed to find joy in the simple and to enjoy what I have. But often times memory is short term. We forget.

Sometimes it takes death to teach us about life, misery to teach us about joy. It is in those times that we realize how much there is to celebrate in life. We must find joy in our daily living and relish it to the fullest. It is there, we must simply look for it.

The average four year old laughs four hundred times a day while adults laugh only fifteen to sixteen times. This should tell us something. Certainly life becomes more serious as we grow up, but that's not reason enough to abandon laughing and enjoying life. Laughter is the sunshine of the soul and the sign of a mentally healthy person, unless you laugh too much. Then your new home will be a private room with padded walls at the funny farm. But I believe people who laugh a lot enjoy life more. Joy is a feeling of grinning inside, and it makes you feel good.

Joy, like happiness, is a by-product of something else. We derive joy from doing certain things or being with particular people. Some major sources of joy in our lives are family, friends, work, and hobbies.

Much joy can be obtained through family relationships. We share our lives, love each other and create pleasant memories. And what about that little bundle of joy, a newborn baby! It has been said that a baby is nature's way of showing you what the world looks like at 2:00 AM. It may not seem joyful at the time, but you would not trade that moment for anything in the world. And they continue to bring joy into your life as they grow up. Kids always brighten up a home. They never turn off the lights!

Friends provide joy and happiness, too. Many times the bond with a friend is just as close as that of a family member. A good friend is a treasure and should be treated as such. A friend knows all of our faults and loves us in spite of them. The nice thing about being imperfect is the joy it brings to others! The most joyful person I know is a close friend and also my pastor, Monsignor Francis. He always has a smile on his face and a song in his heart. He's bubbling and effervescent. It's uplifting just to be around him. Sometimes I wonder if it is normal to be that happy.

If work isn't a joy for you, then you need to do something else. Statistics show that eighty percent of Americans go to jobs they really can not tolerate. Mondays are a hard way to spend one-seventh of your life in a job you don't like. Find other work you enjoy doing or put more joy into what you're doing now. But make some kind of change, even if it is giving up a good paying job! Money does not always bring happiness. A person with three million dollars is no happier than a person with two million!

I was not dissatisfied or unhappy when I left education to become a full time speaker. There were other things I wanted to do in life. I totally enjoy professional speaking and am passionate about it. In fact, I have often confided in friends that even if I were to win the lottery, I would continue doing exactly what I am doing now. I would not change a thing. I have even asked God several times to allow me to win the lottery just to prove that I mean what I am saying. Apparently he is not going to do it, so you will just have to take my word for it.

Hobbies are another excellent way of bringing joy into our lives. They afford us the opportunity to refresh and re-create ourselves. They bring inner peace and joy as we briefly escape the fast pace of daily living. Regardless of whether our hobby is reading, gardening, walking or jogging it should bring us to a state of happiness. Leisure time activities should be filled with joy. We do not lose our joy because we grow old, we grow old because we lose our joy!

If you want more joy in your life, do whatever you are doing with more joy. Pursue it vigorously. It is there for the taking. As you become a more joyful person, you will see yourself in a different light. You will like the person you see. Joy to the world!

Attitudinal Affirmation: "I find joy in everything I do today."

Belief Building Exercise: Carefully scrutinize yesterday's events. Recall the times you were without joy and happiness during the day. Recognize that it was a choice.

Change Producing Action: Promise yourself that you will share your joy and happiness with someone today. Notice their response.

THOUGHTS & ACTION STEPS

K

"Kindness is a universal language in which the blind can see and the deaf can hear."

CHAPTER 11

Kindness

" I shall pass through this world but once. Any good, therefore, that I can do or any kindness that I can show to any human being, let me do it now. Let me not defer nor neglect it for I shall not pass this way again."

Unknown

Kindness is described as being compassionate or generous. In everyday life, we refer to someone like that as being "good hearted." This is a very apt portrayal for that is where kindness originates, in the heart. A kind person is concerned about the feelings and well being of others. He truly cares about them and shows it through word and deed.

The first anniversary of the bombing of the Alfred P. Murrah Federal Building in Oklahoma City was recently observed. To mark the occasion, the governor of Oklahoma and his wife were guests on a popular religious television program. They were asked to recount some of the events of this horrible day. Oklahoma's First Lady shared a touching story. She was working as a volunteer at a receiving station collecting items needed for the victims and workers. A ragged, old car pulled up and the driver said, "I want to help out. I heard that boots are needed for the firemen, so I want to give mine." As she looked in the car, she saw he had nothing on his feet. She also saw that his wife and two children were very poorly clad. They were obviously a family of meager means, but were willing to share what they had. That's kindness in action. Tragedy usually exposes the best in people.

It is important to be kind to others, but we must remember to be kind to ourselves, too. When we do, we recognize that we are a good person with worth and value. We treat ourselves well and we should. We can't pour from an empty cup. Others see in us what we see in ourselves. We receive the kind of treatment we think we deserve. Therefore, the level of our self-esteem will determine how we are treated.

Kindness is a universal language. It is one in which the blind can see and the deaf can hear. Kindness transcends mere words and delves into feelings and emotions. Words come from the head but are filtered through the heart. They carry with them expressions of love, compassion, care, concern and understanding. It is only with the heart that the mind sees clearly. A good rule for going through life is to keep the heart a little softer than the head. Without a doubt, kindness is an attribute of a "people person."

We often hear the phrase, "What goes around comes around." I believe this is absolutely true, especially with kindness. The more kindness we send out, the more comes back to us. It is like looking at the world with soft eyes. So if you have not been the recipient of much kindness lately, perhaps you would do well to examine how you are treating others. It might be quite revealing and help you back on course.

Someone once said that we should commit random acts of kindness, that is, for no particular reason. Deferring to another in traffic, opening a door or taking an elderly neighbor to the supermarket are simple ways of expressing kindness. Can you imagine what kind of world this would be if everyone committed random acts of kindness daily?

One of my favorite ways of doing a good deed anonymously involved the Lake Pontchartrain Causeway, twenty-four miles of bridge over water. At one time, Sue and I had occasion to cross it on a regular basis. The toll for crossing the Causeway was $1.00. You can call it a toll, fee, assessment or a charge. Call it what you want, it's still a tax! And no one really enjoys paying taxes. So I would use this opportunity to do a kind deed and have a little fun at the same time.

As I pulled up to the "toll" booth, I told the attendant, "Here's my dollar and a dollar for my very good friend behind me." And then I would take off across the Causeway! I had no earthly idea who was in that car. Looking in my rear view mirror, I could see the car stop at the booth, arm extend with the money, a short pause, pull back the money and then he would take off. You see, he wanted to find out who his good friend was who had paid his toll.

As he pulls behind me on the Causeway, he is squinting and squirming trying to identify me. Obviously, he can't because he doesn't know me. Then I would speed up a little. Now his curiosity is really getting the best of him. He steps on the gas and pulls along side of me. When he does, I shield my face from him with my left hand. He is beside himself trying to determine who I am. In the meantime, Sue is getting hysterical and shrieking, "Stop it! You're going to get us killed and I don't want to die on this bridge!"

Suddenly, I drop my hand, turn toward the guy and give him a goofy smile. By the bewildered look on his face he must be thinking, "Who is this guy? What is he doing? Why did he pay my toll?" Then I hit the accelerator again and I am on my way. Another small random act of kindness completed. I feel good! And Sue's heart rate has returned to normal by this time! It's a win/win/win situation.

Now, it is easy to be kind to those who are kind to us, but what about those who are not? What about the people who are grouchy, selfish, rude, and have a negative attitude? How will the cycle be broken if we do not make the first move? Reach out to them and "kill'um with kindness." Chances are they are not nice or kind to you because they do not like themselves. Sounds familiar? Of course it does! Because everything begins from within.

Words are lethal so choose them carefully. The old saying, "sticks and stones may break my bones but talk doesn't bother me," is far from true. Words do hurt and their cuts make deep psychological wounds. A gossip has been described as the "knife of the party." Their words cut up a person's character and often do irreparable harm to their self-esteem. This is one of the most unkind acts that could be done to another person. As Dale Carnegie says, "Any fool can criticize, condemn and complain — and most do." A good rule of thumb to follow is, "if you have nothing good to say about someone, then say nothing at all." Blessed is he who has nothing to say and cannot be persuaded to say it!

There are times when the absolute truth could be totally devastating to someone else. Choosing to be tactful by saying little or nothing at all is not, in my opinion, being dishonest. It merely shows your love and compassion for that person. Why hurt their feelings and tarnish or even destroy their self-esteem? Unless the matter is of vital importance, discretion is, indeed, the better part of valor. Diplomacy has been defined as "the art of saying nice doggie, nice doggie, until you can find a big stick." That is not the case here because you are not looking to clobber them. In my mind, you are just handling them with tender loving care. (TLC) What could be kinder than that?

Kindness ought to be a way of life rather than an occasional occurrence. You have an abundance of opportunities every day to perform acts of kindness. Do not overlook any of them. First, be kind to yourself. Then focus on family. Treat others closest to you as you would treat yourself. Taking loved ones for granted is an indication that you are doing the same thing to yourself.

Remember to do the little things. I am particularly referring to the unexpected things, the extras or, as we say in Cajun country, "lagniappe." These include sending a greeting card expressing your love, buying a small gift or giving a well-deserved compliment. It is incredible how much this will do to strengthen a relationship. It is a great investment in people, especially those you love, and you will reap a huge return.

Be sure you are spreading kindness in your work place. Spending from eight to ten hours a day in a place would be torture if you did not care for others. You must do your part. "When you handle yourself, use your head. When you handle others use your heart." That's a good axiom to live by. I saw a sign reading "Through these halls pass the most caring employees in the world" posted above the doorway in a New Orleans hospital. Having that sign up meant the workers there needed to live up to it. It served as a constant reminder of how they should treat one another as well as the patients. They put what they believed in writing for everyone to see so that they could be held accountable. I like that.

Any kindness you show to another person enhances their self-esteem as well as your own. It is such an easy thing to do and costs nothing. Make the effort! Go above and beyond the usual. There is no traffic jam on the extra mile. There are two ways of spreading light: to be the candle or the mirror that reflects it. Choose to light up someone's life today with a kind word or deed. It can change your life and have a profound effect on theirs.

Attitudinal Affirmation: "I perform random acts of kindness everyday."

Belief Building Exercise: Consider all the people with whom you will come in contact tomorrow. Think of something kind you can say or do for each one specifically. Write them down.

Change Producing Action: Actually say and do kind things for those on your list. Notice their response and how you feel.

THOUGHTS & ACTION STEPS

L

"We must learn to love as God loves, unconditionally."

CHAPTER 12

Love

"There are in the end three things that last: faith, hope and love, and the greatest of these is love."

I Corinthians 13:13

Love is probably one of the most misunderstood and misused words in the English language. We use it so loosely that it often loses its significance. For example, I might say I love brownies. Realistically speaking, I can like brownies but I can not love them. So I have misused the word love. I might also say that I loved the movie "Field of Dreams." The same is true with the movie as with the brownies. Love is not involved at all.

The word "love" in its true sense infers a strong emotional attachment to or deep feeling for someone. It is a special bond or relationship that exists among people. Granted, there are various levels of love but none include attachment to things. We would do well to remember that when expressing our feelings. On second thought, there may well be a strong emotional bond between me and those brownies! But that could be the subject of my next book.

We must first learn to love ourselves before we can love others. In essence, that is what self-esteem is — loving ourselves — not a narcissistic, selfish love, but rather one that recognizes our worth and value as a person. Also notice that I said loving ourselves, not being "in love" with ourselves. Being in love with ourselves is conceit and conceit is a disease. It is a strange disease. In fact, it is the only disease I know of that makes everybody sick — except the one who has it! So stay away from it. He who is wrapped up in himself makes a very small package.

During my tenure as principal of Golden Meadow Middle School we implemented the Power of Positive Students Program. It is designed to build self-worth and self-esteem in kids and adults. It is an excellent program and had a tremendous impact on those at school. For the theme song, we selected Whitney Houston's song "The Greatest Love of All." In it she describes the greatest love of all as learning to love yourself. This is so true. Our monthly positive thinking rallies ended with everyone joining hands and singing along with the audio tape. It was very moving and powerful. I believe the message came through very clearly.

Remembering to love yourself is extremely important since the Bible instructs us to love our neighbor as ourselves. This implies that we will love our neighbor only to the extent that we love ourselves. It is very simple — no self love, no love of neighbor. No one wins in this case. It is a lose/lose situation. Conversely, if we love ourselves, that is, see ourselves as having worth, dignity and value, we will see our neighbor the same way and treat him accordingly. The way we feel about ourselves directly affects the way we feel about others. Someone once said to love your neighbor as yourself, but choose your neighborhood.

Love and forgiveness are one. We can't truly love a person if we can not forgive them. Often times we say we forgive someone, but in reality we have not. We tend to bury our hatchets in well marked graves. And when the need arises, we dig them up. Those wounds never heal because we do not forgive. This unforgiveness can very easily lead to hatred. Hating someone is like burning your own house down to get rid of rats. You basically solve the problem but look at what is destroyed in the process.

Holding on to hatred and resentment acts as a tourniquet. It stops the flow of love. Don't let anything cut off your flow of love. It is simply too important. Hatred, like love, has varying degrees as well. Zsa Zsa Gabor said, "I never hated a man enough to give him his diamonds back." I guess that is an individual choice.

We must learn to love as God loves, unconditionally. No strings attached! Granted, this is easier said then done but the effort must be made. To love someone because he/she is rich, attractive, powerful or influential is vain and superficial. This is indicative of low self-esteem. On the contrary, it takes strength to love someone just for who they are without regard for what they have or can do for you.

I have learned some valuable lessons along these lines. Eleven years ago the Lord called me to a prison ministry and my life has not been the same since. At the time, however, I did not want to do it and fought going into prison with every fiber of my being. Why would I want to waste my time with prisoners? There were so many other avenues to pursue. But the Lord was relentless and I reluctantly gave in. I went but I didn't go easy. Thirteen months after receiving the call, I went into Parish Prison in Thibodaux, Louisiana, for the first time. This became a weekly event for seven years.

It proved to be a blessing. I always walked out of the prison feeling uplifted. It mattered to the men that we cared enough to be with them and share our faith. I don't know how much good we did, but I do know some good things happened. One prisoner, Joe, expressed his feelings in a poem he wrote "In Thanks."

In Thanks

I sat alone the other night needing a change
disappointed was I in my life.
But never before have I felt such a change
as the one God gave me that night.

That lonely night I cried alone
covering my tears in vain.
I pleaded for Jesus to give me hope
and deliver me from my pain.

He answered my prayers with a single word
as I sat alone crying in the night.
His word was *love* and though I didn't understand
His presence I could not fight.

He came to me through these bars of despair
soothing my swollen eyes.
Gently relieving the pain in my heart
I thank you, Lord, for that night.

I thank you, Lord, for delivering me
from the foolishness and selfishness I've known.
And I thank you, Lord, for standing beside me
through your love I know I've grown.

I can only pray you give me strength
to push temptation aside.
And guide me through these troubled times
and strengthen the bonds of my life.

O Lord, I thank you for being there
beside me when I needed you most.
And can only promise in return of your love
my heart forever will be your host.

Thank You Lord

This poem as well as others helped me realize that we were instruments of God's love. That is why I needed to be there. It is God's will for me and what I must do. I know that in my heart. I also know that there but for the grace of God go I.

From Parish prison, I became involved in a national prison ministry called "Kairos" initiated at Louisiana State Penitentiary at Angola. Kairos is a Greek work meaning "God's special time." This is even more powerful because of its three and one-half day retreat format. Forty-two prisoners are exposed to a highly structured but spirit-filled weekend. It was amazing to witness the gradual transformation occurring in these hardened men. Hearts were softened, walls torn down, and tears shed as they accepted Christ in their life. It was awesome!

The closing ceremony afforded each prisoner the opportunity to share with the Kairos community what he had received from the weekend. The recurring theme was love, love, love. Here is a sample of the testimony given.

> "I came here when I was twenty with a life sentence—that was twenty-six years ago. I ain't got nobody — no wife or children or parents or family. But if I die here, I will never forget that there was three and one-half days when I was loved."

> "I found what I'd been looking for all my life. I didn't

> know what it was; it was love."
>
> "I never believed, but became a believer. I give God thanks for being asked to come. I may be in prison forever, but I'm free."

I am not attempting to make a case for criminals or to be soft on crime. I am simply trying to see these men as human beings and children of God. The reality is that God loves them just as much as He loves you and me. And I believe it is possible to love the sinner without loving or condoning the sin. Many prisoners have never been loved or have been abandoned by their family. They are not only prisoners of the judicial system, but prisoners of poor self-esteem and lack of love, too. They are overwhelmed when they receive unconditional love from Kairos team members during the retreat weekend. For many, it is the first time they have experienced that kind of love — and it makes a difference.

Love is a powerful emotion that can touch hearts and change lives, even at Angola, once known as the bloodiest prison in the South. If it can affect this hostile environment, imagine the kind of world we could have if we made an honest effort to love one another every day. It is certainly possible but we need to get started.

Why not start by giving hugs? Hugs make the perfect gift. One fits all sizes and they are easy to exchange. I like to hug. (I almost said I love to hug, but after the dissertation on love and the brownies at the beginning of the chapter, I dare not!) Once we have met, you are eligible to be hugged from then on. It is a great way to express affection, friendship and love. Like Jackie DeShannon's popular song in the seventies said, "What the world needs now is love, sweet love. Not just for some but for everyone."

Attitudinal Affirmation: "I love myself and everyone else."

Belief Building Exercise: Identify the ways you could show love for yourself. If you have difficulty, ask for help and love yourself enough to receive it.

Change Producing Action: Use these ways daily in order to see your worth and value. Then start showing love to others with a hug.

M

"I believe everyone is searching for a role model, not a hero."

CHAPTER 13

MODEL

"If you always live with those who are lame, you will yourself learn to limp."

LATIN PROVERB

A model serves as an example and is someone to be copied or imitated. Modeling is the process through which we gradually take on the characteristics of someone else. To pursue this line of thought, positive modeling is the act of presenting attitudes, behaviors and habits which are worthy of imitation.

Modeling is one of the most common and powerful forms of learning — so powerful in fact that many psychologists believe that mere association among family members has just as much influence on the development of attitude and behavior as does genetics. Often times as a principal I wondered why a student acted a certain way — then I met the parents. The apple doesn't fall far from the tree.

I would like to address this issue from two perspectives. First, from the standpoint that each of us serves as a role model to others and secondly, that we could have people in our lives that we can emulate.

Regardless, we serve as role models every day. We affect and influence other people. The kind of role model we are depends on the level of our self-esteem. Obviously, the higher our self-esteem, the more positive role model we can be.

Would you be proud if a friend or loved one imitated your behavior? If not, perhaps a self inventory would be in order to determine what needs to be changed.

As kids, we all had heroes. These were people we imitated and not always for the right reasons. They included athletes, movie stars and rock and roll singers. (The last one is a dead giveaway for my age.) We never looked at their character or values; our only concern was how well they performed. And on that basis, we would have given our all to be just like them.

But there is a distinct difference between a hero and a role model. Only recently did it become clear to me, and it came through Mickey Mantle, the great center fielder of the New York Yankees. My favorite baseball team growing up was the Cleveland Indians. The Yankees and the Indians were big rivals and perennially battled for the American League pennant. The Yankees usually won, and I despised them for that.

Mickey Mantle was the star during the Yankee dynasty. He had the looks, talent and charisma to fill the mold of a hero. He loomed larger than life. Although the Yankees were the enemy, I greatly admired Mantle. But I was only looking at superficial things — his speed, power and graceful movement in the outfield. I knew very little about him as a person and, at that time, didn't care.

His life-style, which included heavy drinking, caused serious health problems in later life. Just this past year, Mantle underwent a liver transplant. At a news conference following his surgery, a reporter brought up the subject of his status as a hero. Mantle responded soberly and almost apologetically, "I may have been a hero, but I certainly was not a role model."

That is when the difference between the two really struck

me. At this point he realized that, as a ball player, he had squandered the opportunity as well as the responsibility to serve as a positive role model for kids. He did not want youngsters to follow in his footsteps, so he openly told his story cautioning kids to avoid the evils of alcohol and drugs. It took courage to admit his mistake.

The second verse of Whitney Houston's song, "The Greatest Love Of All" alluded to in the previous chapter, begins with "everybody's searching for a hero, people need someone to look up to." I believe everyone is searching for a role model, not a hero. We all need someone to admire, respect, and emulate — someone who will have a positive influence on us. In no way does this mean we should allow ourselves to become their clone. We should simply take the best of what they offer and incorporate it into our lives.

By the same token, when you are exactly like someone else you lose your individuality. You are not one in million, you are one of a kind. There never has been, is now or ever will be anyone on the face of this earth exactly like you. I remember telling Sue one day, "Do you know that I'm unique, special and one of a kind? Do you know there is no one else like me in the entire world? Do you realize that?" She looked at me out of the corner of her eye and said, "I knooow! And I thank God every day for that!" What a great sense of humor! So be yourself, but be the best you that you can be. There are few things harder to put up with than the annoyance of a good example!

Who are the role models in your life? What attracts you to them? Identify those qualities and make certain they are worthy of imitation. If not, maybe you need to look elsewhere. You need to be inspired by the right people. This will help your self-esteem and overall development as a person.

As you serve as a positive role model for others, you will continually be strengthened by the influence of the important people in your life. You may find it becomes easier to be a positive role model as you allow yourself to be strengthened. There's an old saying, "If you ain't got it, you can't give it."

We serve as role models everyday. Hopefully, it is a positive one. Be sure there is no conflict between your words and actions. People more attention pay to what you do than what you say. You will lose your credibility if your words and actions do not coincide. Closely monitor your behavior, dress, language and non-verbal communication to determine what kind of messages you are sending. If you have children, this is an especially tough challenge since they mirror your attitudes and beliefs so clearly. Ask yourself this question: What kind of world would this world be, if everyone in it were just like me? Walk your talk and you will be on solid ground and boost your self-esteem in the process.

Attitudinal Affirmation: "I am a good example for all those with whom I come in contact today."

Belief Building Exercise: After an inventory of the people in your life, make a list of your role models. Identify the qualities you admire in them.

Change Producing Action: Within the next few days, contact these people and tell them that you consider them to be your role models. Also let them know why.

THOUGHTS & ACTION STEPS

N

"To nurture is to provide encouragement and support."

CHAPTER 14

NURTURE

"A candle loses nothing of its light by lighting another candle."

JAMES KELLER

To nurture means to develop or nourish. It is helping someone or something to grow and become more than it already is. Nurturing is a gradual process requiring time and the ingredients necessary for growth to occur. We nurture ourselves as well as others.

Nurturing takes place best in a positive climate. William Rasberry, a former columnist with the Washington Post, describes a positive climate as a "nurturing cocoon." In this scenario, the ugly caterpillar enters the cocoon and emerges as a beautiful butterfly. The cocoon provided the environment necessary for the transformation to take place. Its warmth and nourishment encouraged the growth. The same kind of nurturing environment is required for our self-esteem to be enhanced. This atmosphere of acceptance empowers us to feel good about ourselves and to interact with others in a positive way.

To nurture is to provide encouragement and support. All need this regardless of the current level of his/her self-esteem. Sue has always encouraged me and is a vital part of my support system. Whether I was seeking a promotion in the school system or preparing for a difficult speaking engagement, she was always in my corner. And I appreciate it. I recall leaving to do a keynote for a school district in Florida recently when Sue provided a bit of sage advice. She said, "Look Curt, tomorrow when you're addressing those good folks in Jackson County, don't try to be witty, charming or intellectual. Just be yourself!" How much support does one man deserve?

Nurturing plays a significant role in the Kairos Prison Ministry. After the retreat weekend, the men are encouraged to join small prayer and share groups that meet weekly. The purpose is to nurture the development of their spiritual growth. A reunion is held the first Saturday of each month for all the men who have made a Kairos weekend. The prisoners are responsible for organizing and leading the two hour meeting. They select the leader, scripture reading, songs and those who will give testimony. The idea is to have them become self sufficient. The role of the volunteers at the reunion is one of nurturing through support and encouragement.

Appreciation is a form of nurturing and an important psychological need. According to one psychologist, about ninety percent of what we do daily is done out of the desire to be appreciated. We do not mind busting our back getting something done, but we would like to be acknowledged for it. Bob Hope was asked why he did not retire and go fishing. His response was classic, "Fish don't applaud." Affirmation is necessary for building our self-esteem and sense of self-worth.

Giving compliments is a great way of nurturing others, too. Compliment liberally but only when it is deserved. Accept a compliment by maintaining eye contact and simply saying, "Thank you." The inability to accept praise is a sign of low self-esteem. That person will refute the compliment by demeaning its value because of feelings of unworthiness. So when someone offers a compliment and you know they are sincere, accept it! Savor it! Man does not live on bread alone, he needs a little buttering up every now and then.

True nurturing is learning to enjoy the path, the process, the journey toward your dream. Success is a journey, not a destination. It is achieved not in one giant leap, but in many small steps. Nurturing helps to keep the process going. It is critical to recognize the small successes along the way. Learn to enjoy them. This provides the nourishment needed to continue striving for one's dream.

A practical means of nourishment is to maintain a "success list." It is comprised of congratulatory cards, letters, honors, newspaper clippings and anything else indicative of something you have achieved. When you are down or discouraged, go to your success list. Browsing through the items will lift your spirits. You will realize that what you are now experiencing is just a temporary setback. It will give you the strength and courage to go on. I call this a "nurturing moment."

I have done this for many years now. My success list consists of a variety of mementos contained in several photo albums. I particularly enjoy reading a card or letter from someone relating that something I said in one of my talks made a difference in their life or workplace. My favorite is from an English teacher in Meigs County, Tennessee. She actually wrote the letter to Sue. This one I keep in my brief case and often read it in flight enroute to a speaking engagement. It is affirming for me to know that what I am doing is important and it keeps my batteries charged, too. I assure you it is very powerful and effective. I highly recommend it.

When nurturing we would do well to remember the Serenity Prayer: "God grant me the serenity to accept the things I cannot change, courage to change the things I can and the wisdom to know the difference." It would do little good for us to beat up on ourselves for something beyond our control. Of course this brings to mind a story.

Jimmy, of DeMoss Photographers, and I were chatting in my office at Golden Meadow Middle school before he began taking student pictures. He was relating how parents can be very particular about their children's pictures and want them to look perfect. He said one parent refused to buy her child's pictures because she was dissatisfied with them. Jimmy asked what was the problem, and her comment was, "This just does not look like my daughter. It doesn't do her justice!" Jimmy said, "Curt, that picture captured her daughter to a tee. There was absolutely nothing wrong with it." After a few more exchanges he said, "I told her in frustration, 'Madam, DeMoss Photographers cannot undo what God has done!'"

Nurturing others requires that we be gentle and patient. There is nothing in the world stronger than gentleness. The tenderness provided shows the love, care and compassion needed for growth and support. Give the process time to work. If you plant a tree, you don't keep pulling it out by the roots to see if it is growing. Gentleness requires a certain strength to allow the one you support to make mistakes and flounder. You're familiar with the saying, "Give a man a fish and you feed him for a day. Teach a man to fish and you get rid of him on weekends!"

No one is an island. We need each other as well as all the love, support and encouragement we can get. This nurtures our self-esteem. But it needs time. The story about the Chinese Bamboo Tree illustrates this point. The seeds for the tree are planted, watered, fertilized and nurtured. At the end of one year, nothing happens. We continue to water, fertilize and nurture during the second year and still nothing happens. This procedure is repeated for two more years with the same results.

Sometime during the fifth year, however, the bamboo tree grows ninety feet in six weeks. I pose the obvious question. Did the bamboo tree grow ninety feet in six weeks, or did it grow ninety feet in five years? The answer, too, is obvious. Had it not been for the planting, watering, fertilizing and nurturing during the first four years, the tree could not have experienced the growth spurt during the fifth year. The same is true concerning our self-esteem. The level of our self-esteem five years from now depends upon the amount of nurturing we provide during this time. So be good to yourself, plant the seeds, then provide the water and fertilizer. (Watch the fertilizer!) And then — nurture, nurture, nurture! Watch your self-esteem grow!

Attitudinal Affirmation: "I receive nurturing for my mind, body and spirit everyday."

Belief Building Exercise: Identify two things you can add to your daily routine that will nurture your self-esteem.

Change Producing Action: Start doing those two things tomorrow and continue until they become a habit.

O

"The optimist doesn't go through life with blinders denying the existence of problems, he simply refuses to let them defeat him."

CHAPTER 15

Optimism

"One of the things I learned the hard way was that it doesn't pay to get discouraged. Keeping busy and making optimism a way of life can restore your faith in yourself."

Lucille Ball

Optimism is the assurance and confidence that things will work out right. It is looking on the bright side of things and none ever injured their eyesight by doing that. It is also looking for the good in everything and refusing to be discouraged or dwell on it when life seems to be dealing you a lousy hand. Optimism is a choice and it is within our power to decide if that is the way we want to live life.

Optimism is closely related to attitude. People who have a positive attitude are usually very optimistic. They understand that a situation may not turn out the way they would like, but they focus on the good and move on. They continually ask, "What else can go right?" The pessimist, however, cannot help but see what went wrong, or even worse, what might go wrong. They wallow in self-pity and misery. "Woe is me" is their theme song. They throw pity-parties frequently and try to get as many party-goers to attend as possible. Why? Because misery loves company.

Many distinctions have been made between an optimist and a pessimist, and the good news is that you are going to have more. Here goes! An optimist believes he will go to heaven. A pessimist fears he will spend eternity next to an optimist. It would serve him right. But at least they are both in heaven.

A dandruff commercial aired a few years ago on television. The actor said, "All my life I've had this terrible cloud hanging over my head." He was referring, of course, to dandruff. But that's the lot of a pessimist. He walks around all day with this dark, storm-like cloud hanging over him expecting the worst to happen. He is inviting trouble and misfortune into his life. And the invitation will be gladly accepted. More will be discussed about this in the chapter on expectations, but for the moment, suffice it to say that he is flirting with disaster. A pessimist is someone who can look at the land of milk and honey and see only calories and cholesterol.

An optimist, on the other hand, expects the best. The attitude is one of, "The difficult we do immediately. Miracles take a little longer." He sees a task at hand, pounces on it and expects it to be successful. Failure or discouragement is never an option. He moves forward with hope and enthusiasm always expecting the best. He is like the person who saves the seed catalog pictures to compare with the flowers and vegetables he actually grows.

Someone jokingly described an optimist as someone who tells you to cheer up when things are going his way. That may well be the case sometimes. But the optimistic person will continue to be cheerful and happy even when he is having difficulties. That is his nature, to see the good in everything and to focus on it. A young boy brought his report card home to his father. His first glance at the card revealed that his son had received four F's and one D. After careful examination of the report card his father exclaimed, "Son, I see what the problem is. You're concentrating too hard on one subject!"

Optimism is like a forest fire — you can smell it for miles before you see it burning. One can sense that same kind of confidence and enthusiasm burning within an optimistic person. She will not be denied the opportunity nor the success. She knows good things will happen and proceeds with vigor. She is excited about life and living. She is the one who begins putting on her shoes when she hears the speaker say, "And now in conclusion."

A psychologist at the University of Pennsylvania has proven that optimists are more successful than equally talented pessimists — in business, education, sports and politics. This should come as no surprise. They believe that they will always succeed no matter what the odds. Success is inevitable with that kind of determination and belief. A pessimist, on the other hand, complains about the noise when opportunity knocks.

If ever we needed a spirit of optimism in this country it is now. A ballooning national debt, a shrinking Social Security fund, uncertain changes in the delivery of healthcare — all contribute to legitimate concerns for the future. But what will an attitude of gloom and doom change? Absolutely nothing! Or if it does, it will only make it worse. The optimist doesn't go through life with blinders denying the existence of problems, he simply refuses to let them defeat him. He maintains a cheerful spirit and does what he can to make things better.

His hope is not without foundation, though. Look at how dismal and bleak times have been in the past. And yet, this "look for the silver lining" attitude has always pulled us through. And it will again. It's like the teenage driver pointing to the crushed fender on the family car and saying, "Great news, Dad! You haven't been pouring all those insurance payments down the drain!" All of those optimism payments we have been making will not go down the drain either. They will return handsome dividends and make us glad we paid the premiums.

Are you an optimist or a pessimist? Be honest with yourself. Realize that a tough-minded optimism will empower you to approach the twenty-first century with hope and enthusiasm. Optimism is like fly paper — you can't help getting stuck to it. And that's O.K. because you want it to stay with you. Searching for the good in life and in others will lead you to find the good in yourself. And that will boost your self-esteem. Go for it!

Attitudinal Affirmation: "I am positively more positive everyday."

Belief Building Exercise: Recall to mind this week's events. Determine which ones you viewed with optimism. Then look for any that you viewed negatively, and see it in the same optimistic way. Pay attention to what your body is telling you and the way you feel. Notice a shift?

Change Producing Action: Resolve to be an optimist today regardless of what happens. Look for the silver lining in any negative event and keep your focus on it.

THOUGHTS & ACTION STEPS

P

"We imprison ourselves with self-limiting thoughts and beliefs."

CHAPTER 16

Potential

"No human being ever learns to live until he has awakened to the dormant powers within him."

William James

Potential refers to what is possible as opposed to what is actual. We have within us, the capability of becoming more than we presently are. God has blessed each one of us with a vast amount of inherent talent and ability, and yet, human potentiality remains a mystery.

People are the only living thing in nature that does not grow to its full potential. Every other living thing does. That is because we choose not to. Psychologists tell us that the average person develops, at best, only ten percent of his potential. We think we are operating on all eight cylinders when, in reality, it's less than one. What a waste of human resources! Environmentalists rant about wasting our natural resources, and in many cases, rightly so. We waste our natural resources by using them up. We waste our human resources by not using them at all. That is the real tragedy!

I mentioned earlier that I am a volunteer in the Kairos Prison Ministry at Louisiana State Penitentiary at Angola. I recall walking in my first time and seeing all the physical signs of incarceration — the cold steel bars, the tall fences topped with rolls of sharp razor wire, the armed guards perched high in their watch towers monitoring every move. And then I suddenly realized that many of us are prisoners just like these men, not in a state institution, but within the walls of our own minds. We imprison ourselves with self-limiting thoughts and beliefs — and these self-imposed, psychological limitations are just as real and confining as the physical ones at Angola. They keep us shackled and stop us from reaching our potential.

Having potential and not developing it is like having an oil well in your back yard and, either you don't know it is there or you don't drill it. Either way it does nothing for you. When you identify your talents and develop them you can create your life in such a way as to go beyond your wildest dream. There are two ways to climb an oak tree. One way is to simply go out and climb the tree. The other is to plant an acorn, sit on it and wait. Both will work, but one is a lot easier and more effective. If you sit on your talent, you waste your potential.

As a people we seem content to come to the end of our lives and contribute to the richest place on earth. That being the cemetery! Why? Because therein lies all the untapped potential, unfulfilled dreams, unsung songs, unwritten books and lost job opportunities. This talent pool is lost forever because of fear and the unwillingness to risk.

My favorite writer, Og Mandino, says that we should be called human becomings instead of human beings because the term human being implies that we are a finished product — that this is all we are going to be. And that's not true! We are always in the process of becoming all that God intended us to be and all that we're capable of becoming. From womb to tomb we must be striving to reach our potential.

God supplies us with all the talent, skill and ability necessary for success. We must provide the desire, motivation and commitment. We are stakeholders in this endeavor and must do our part. A tourist was driving in the country and came to a beautiful farm. Said the tourist, "My, my, you and the Lord have certainly done a magnificent job with this farm." The farmer replied, "Yea, but you should have seen it when the Lord had it by himself." Developing our potential and achieving success are our responsibility.

We can not become what we need to be by remaining what we are. Charles Dubois said, "The important thing is this: to be able to sacrifice at any moment what we are for what we could become." The problem is we don't want to let go of what we now have. Remaining tight-fisted prevents us from grabbing on to something new, and it stifles our growth.

"The Monkey Hunt" story illustrates this point quite clearly. In certain parts of the world where monkeys are hunted, they are sometimes captured with a very simple trap. A coconut is tied to a tree with a chain. A hole is made in the coconut just big enough to allow a monkey to put his hand through the opening. Then a walnut is placed in the coconut, and the trapper leaves.

Along comes a monkey, and anxious to have the walnut, he reaches in and grabs it. With the walnut in his closed fist, he can not take his hand out of the coconut — but he will not surrender the walnut, either. As a result of this, the monkey will still be sitting there when the trapper returns to retrieve him. Because the monkey does not have the ability to reason, he does not understand that he must let go of the walnut in order to avoid being captured and remain free. We, as rational human beings, refuse to let go of what is in our hand just like the monkey. The price we pay is the freedom lost to reach our potential. So quit monkeying around and let go!

We often say if we had someone else's money, good looks,

intelligence or body build that we could do great things. Well, that is not necessarily so. There were two lumberjacks who were good friends. One weighed 150 pounds and was 5'5" tall. His buddy was a monster of a man. He was 6'6" tall and weighed 280 pounds. The little lumberjack told his buddy, "Man, if I was as big and strong as you, I'd go in those woods and grab the biggest, " baddest," meanest bear I could find and turn him every way but loose!" The big lumberjack looked at him and said, "You know, partner, there's a lot of little bears in those woods, too!"

It's time we stop griping about what we don't have and focus on what we do. The idea is to find a task or challenge commensurate with our ability. Our success is not measured by what we have done in relation to what others have done. Our success is measured by what we have done as compared to what we are capable of doing. The only competition is within ourselves, not with others. That is important to remember. When we take what God has given us, develop it and use it; we find that life becomes more fulfilling.

William Shakespeare said, "We may know what we are, but know not what we may be." Only time and the continuous development of our potential will provide the answer. God knows but He's not talking. Anyone can count the number of seeds in an apple, but only God knows how many apples are in a seed.

What fears are keeping you prisoner? What psychological limitations are holding you hostage? Until you decide to free yourself from this bondage and unlock your potential, you are every bit as much a prisoner as the inmates at Louisiana State Penitentiary. So break out of the prison of your mind! The choice is yours: to be a prisoner of fear — or to unlock the power of potential. Which one will you choose?

Attitudinal Affirmation: "I am open to my potential and I develop it everyday."

Belief Building Exercise: Ask yourself the question, "If I was assured that I would be successful in any endeavor, guaranteed not to fail, what would I do?" How would I use my potential to do this?

Change Producing Action: List the steps to do it and begin.

Q

"There is a distinct difference between a standard of living and a quality of life."

CHAPTER 17

Quality

"The quality of life within a community is dependent upon the quality of each individual living and working within that community."

Mayor Ernest "Dutch" Morial

Quality is a word we hear often today. And after all is said and done, unfortunately, more is said than done. We like to talk about quality, but many times lip service seems to take precedence over action. Quality means insuring excellence. In business and industry it means meeting or exceeding customer needs and expectations. Terminology has changed from Quality Assurance to Continuous Quality Improvement, and the process has changed somewhat, but the ultimate outcome is still the same – improvement. This concept can be applied to our lives as well.

We want and expect quality wherever we go, but the meaning of quality may differ among people. A patron went into a restaurant and began to order breakfast. Said he to the waitress, "I want two fried eggs dripping with grease, burnt toast, frozen butter and cold coffee." She replied, "Sir, I couldn't possibly serve that to you!" "Sure you can," he said, "You did yesterday!" We should be constantly aware of quality, whether it be in a product, service or our own lives.

Note that there is a distinct difference between a standard of living and a quality of life. The former implies attainment of a certain amount of money and goods, while the latter relates to the possession of peace, love, happiness, contentment, etc. Attempting to raise one's standard of living by acquiring "stuff" does not mean that one will improve the quality of life. It never has and never will. It simply means one has "stuff!"

Vince Lombardi said, "The quality of a person's life is in direct proportion to his commitment to excellence, regardless of his chosen field of endeavor." Striving for excellence is an on-going process. The race for quality has no finish line.

One aspect of living a quality life is to be "on purpose." It is knowing why you are on this earth and spending your life fulfilling it. It is your reason for existing. I remember many years ago saying that I could retire immediately and be perfectly content playing golf every day the rest of my life. At that time I was afflicted with the paralyzing disease, "golf on the brain."

I would rush to the golf course every day. So much so that my first accident ever was at a bridge on the way to the course. The other car was driven by a friend who was headed there, too. Now there was a Kodak moment — two fanatical golfers headed for the same place at the same time. Disaster! That should have given me a clue!

But that was when I was young and foolish. Now that I am old and foolish, I realize that there is more to life than chasing a little white ball through grass, water and sand. Are we having fun yet? (I don't mean to offend any golfers, but they are probably on the golf course anyhow and not reading this.)

I was still playing a few rounds of golf every month when I retired from the school system to begin my speaking career.

Being a very time consuming game, I soon realized that golf interfered with my purpose and mission. I knew then that golf was expendable — and it was. I've played one round in the last three years and that was a special Lions Club function on July 4th.

I don't miss the game at all, but I do miss the camaraderie with my buddies. Actually, I am surprised one of my friends, Ray C., still plays as much golf as he does because he is, well, henpecked. I discovered that a few years ago while he and I were talking in his living room. Ray C.'s wife, Brenda, handed him his jacket. He looked up at her and asked, "Am I cold or am I going somewhere?"

I now invest time developing my speaking career and working in community activities. I have come to understand that I must have something meaningful going on in my life at all times. I was so wrong when I thought golf could achieve this. I believe I am now "on purpose."

Quality of life implies balance between work and play. Obviously we must work in order to provide for our needs, but it should not be all consuming. Workaholics are out of balance and need to make adjustments in their life. I know a workaholic. He starts drinking every time you mention the word work. Remember, all work and no play makes Johnny a dull boy. Taking time to play or re-create energizes and helps you to be more productive. Stephen Covey, author of The 7 Habits of Highly Effective People, calls this "sharpening the saw." This means getting away from your regular work routine in order to refresh yourself. Failure to do so can result in burnout. Now, I know some folks who are claiming burn out, but that's impossible, because they were never lit!

There are some who would argue that they must work

constantly to meet the financial demands of daily living. There is some merit to this but they should remember that money is not everything — there are mutual funds, property investments and condominiums! But I can understand their concern. I came from a very poor background having been born and reared on a sugar cane plantation. I started with nothing — and still have most of it! Being poor is an attitude. Being broke is a condition that most of us experience at one time or another. Recognize the difference.

We have lost quality in many things, from the air we breathe to the water we drink and even the music we enjoy. What ever happened to the music that was popular in my prime, music that had meaning and substance? Like Oliver Morgan's "Who Shot The La La?" with the memorable line, "sitting here in la la waiting for my ya ya, uh huh, uh huh." Now there are lyrics you can really sink your teeth into! Ahhh, those oldies but goodies! Gone but not forgotten.

Regardless, each New Year I set goals in various areas of my life. The plan is well balanced but the key is to pull it off. I have found that one area out of kilter in my life is recreation. As I mentioned earlier, I no longer play golf, or tennis for that matter. Father Scott has called several times to play tennis but I had already jogged, and as I told him, I can not do two physical activities in one day. It is either a sign of old age or laziness, take your pick.

But we will get together soon. And when we do, I will need to remember that there is a fine line between warming up and burning out. I do jog three times a week, but there is no social aspect to it. It does keep me fit and feeling good, though.

Sue bowls in a weekly league for recreation. She is very skilled and committed as well. Very little interferes with

Tuesday night bowling. In fact, I have often remarked that if I die on Tuesday, the wake would be held after 10:00 PM or early Wednesday morning. But since I plan on living to be at least one hundred, I don't foresee a problem.

According to Earl Nightingale, "The person, business or institution that insists on quality will wind up on top of the pile sooner or later." It is a funny thing about life, if you refuse to accept anything but the best, you very often get it. There is no substitute for quality or excellence. And it starts on the inside. Remember the TV commercial, "At Zenith, the quality goes in before the name goes on." That's true with us, too.

Several years ago I determined my mission, vision and values in an effort to gain perspective and pursue a quality life. Although it is a personal document, I would like to share it with you and encourage you to craft your own.

My Mission

I am in the speaking profession to help people achieve a better way to live and be more productive by recognizing their self-worth, improving their self-esteem, developing a positive attitude and learning how to set and reach goals. I want to make a difference in people's lives through word and example.

My Vision

To become a nationally and internationally known speaker and author and be highly sought after for conferences and conventions.

My Values

I strongly believe in and am committed to:
*Quality and excellence in speaking and in life
*Honesty and integrity with each client
*Being "customer friendly"
*Being totally prepared for each engagement
*Always delivering more than is expected
*Providing value equal to or greater than the compensation
*Being worthy of trust in all situations
*Treating all people with dignity and respect
*Speaking as a privilege and an honor
*Helping other speakers as much as possible
*Continuing personal and professional growth

I had occasion to share my mission, vision and values with the assistant superintendent of Lafourche Parish Schools while discussing an upcoming project. We have been friends for years. Perry read it then looked at me and said, "Curt, this is you." His comment was affirming.

So how do you live a quality life? One way is to decide what you would like to have said in your eulogy, then live your life accordingly. Again, this is related to one of Stephen Covey's 7 habits called "begin with the end in mind." Knowing how you want to be remembered clearly tells you the kind of life you must live in order for it to become a reality. Living a quality life will make a difference for you and others as well. Your self-esteem will increase in proportion to the quality of your life.

Attitudinal Affirmation: "I have peace, love, joy and contentment in my life."

Belief Building Exercise: Write your mission, vision and values. Post them in a place where they can remind you to stay "on purpose."

Change Producing Action: Share your list with family members or a few friends. Ask for feedback from them to determine if you are congruent with your mission, vision and values statement.

R

"We may not be responsible for the things that happen to us, but we are responsible for the way we behave when they do happen."

CHAPTER 18

Responsibility

"The price of greatness is responsibility."
Winston Churchill

"It's not my fault." That is a frequent reply when something goes wrong. And in some cases it may be true. But more often than not, we are quick to point the finger at someone else in an effort to avoid taking responsibility. That is playing the "blame game." We would do well to remember that when pointing a finger at others, there are three fingers pointing right back at us. And that is usually where the responsibility lies, with us. Ralph Waldo Emerson said, "We may not be responsible for the things that happen to us, but we are responsible for the way we behave when they do happen."

Technically, responsibility means being trustworthy, reliable and dependable. Yet, it has come to mean much more than that. Many people see it today as response-ability, that is, the ability to choose your response in any given situation or set of circumstances. There is a brief time lag between a stimulus and our response to it. Once an action takes place, we have the opportunity to choose how we are going to respond. This dispels or, at the very least, reduces the notion of victimization. Since we have a choice, we have assumed responsibility for the outcome. We can choose to be the master of our destiny or the victim of our destiny. Many people today whine about the poor hand life has dealt them. We have a choice. We can complain and feel sorry for ourselves or we can take charge and do something to change it. Taking the hand life has dealt us and making the most of it is response-ability and a sign of maturity. To grow old is mandatory, to mature is optional.

It is much easier to blame someone else instead of accepting responsibility for our own actions. I was guilty of that just a few years ago. As previously alluded to, I had planned to pursue a speaking career after finishing thirty years in education. Feeling I was being led by the Lord to begin now, I "retired" from the educational system after only twenty-four years.

When my speaking career did not develop as quickly as I thought it would, I became very frustrated and angry — at God. I felt that he had led me on this path and then abandoned me. It was much easier to blame Him than to accept responsibility for my own actions. It was my choice and decision, yet I refused to accept it. It was definitely a valley experience and undoubtedly the lowest point of my life. It was at this time that I stayed away from prison ministry work for one year. I simply kept blaming God for what was not right in my life. It couldn't be my fault, right?

My frustration and anger developed into a deep bitterness, and I fell into a state of despair. I felt alone and isolated. Although I resisted returning to prison ministry work, I felt compelled to share my experience of high expectations, big disappointment and low morale with the inmates. In the process I felt cleansed and relieved. I had finally owned up to my decision and taken responsibility for my actions. It was a healing experience to share my feelings of frustration.

Fortunately, things have improved considerably since then. Through this episode, however, I will discover if God really has a sense of humor when I arrive at the Pearly Gates. I had better have some good answers because I know He will have some great questions!

Each human being on this planet must take total responsibility for his own inner development. We have the responsibility to nurture, develop and fulfill the life God has given us. Life is a precious gift, we are only stewards. We are accountable to God for what we do with our life and all of our gifts. Developing and using those gifts is answering the call to be responsible.

Some people see responsibility as boring, but it is actually very exciting. The more we see we are responsible for our life, the more influence we have in directing it in a more satisfying way. That is when we begin to take charge of ourselves. At this point we are empowered.

With leadership comes responsibility, for others as well as ourselves. We have their well-being in our hands and must exercise good judgment. Many times it is necessary to humble ourselves and ask that which we do not know. But some don't know how or simply refuse. Moses wandered around in the desert for forty years. His journey, however, does have great historical significance. It was the first recorded instance of a man refusing to ask for directions! We might want to consider soliciting the help of others if we don't want to always take the scenic route through life.

As I speak, I am constantly traveling to new places. I don't hesitate to stop and ask for directions when I feel like I am off course. I don't want to waste time and, furthermore, they won't remember me. This position caused some embarrassment for me on one occasion. I was looking for a hotel in New Orleans and had been unable to locate it after driving in the area for awhile. Upon stopping and asking a bystander, he replied, "You're right in front of it." I sheepishly responded,

"That's just what I thought!"

We should carry out our responsibility to the fullest even though it may not have a direct effect upon us or our loved ones. It is an indication of maturity and caring. A sign above each workbench on the production line of a television manufacturing plant reads: "Careful, this may be the one you get." The fact you are not in the market for a television set at the moment should not diminish your responsibility for providing the best.

Let us begin to choose our responses carefully in all situations. By so doing we are accepting responsibility for ourselves and our actions. This acceptance in turn allows us to be in charge of our lives. Let us be the master of our destiny by assuming responsibility for our lives. Taking charge feels good and will help us to feel good about ourselves! The poem Invictus by William Ernest Henley reminds us that, "It matters not how straight the gate, how charged with punishments the scroll. I am the master of my fate, I am the captain of my soul."

Attitudinal Affirmation: "I accept full responsibility for my words and actions."

Belief Building Exercise: Carefully examine today's events. Decide if you have avoided taking responsibility for an action or situation. Determine why.

Change Producing Action: Count to ten before responding to any situation today. This will give you the time necessary to make a wise decision. Accept responsibility for the outcome.

THOUGHTS & ACTION STEPS

S

"We make a living by what we get, we make a life by what we give."

CHAPTER 19

SERVICE

"There is no higher religion than human service. To work for the common good is the highest creed."
ALBERT SCHWEITZER

Service is giving with absolutely no desire to receive in return. It is one of our deepest joys and is a privilege, not a chore. In essence, it is saying that our life is blessed and we have a desire to share that blessing with others.

The only things we can take with us when we leave this world are the things we have given away. The things we do for self are gone when we are gone, but the things we do for others remain as our legacy. What a powerful thought! What kind of legacy do we want to leave? How do we want to be remembered?

I have been a member of the Golden Meadow Lions Club since 1972 and am still active today. It is a service organization which focuses primarily on sight conservation and helping handicapped children. I have had the privilege of serving in various leadership positions and participating in numerous service activities. I recall making the statement many years ago that all I wanted on my headstone was, "Here lies an S.O.B. who cared." Twenty-four years later I still want the same inscription, but I would like to have it stated just a little bit more eloquently.

There are many and varied ways of serving. Just look around your community and instantly you will see a need. When the server is ready, the service appears. When you find something that resonates within, that makes you feel warm, full and satisfied, you will know that this is your area of service. The challenge is not so much finding some cause which suits your talent and temperament, but looking and being open to the possibilities.

When you volunteer to make your community a better place to live, your rewards will be in direct proportion to your service. Rewards follow service. You do not serve for that reason, but that is the natural outcome. Even though your intention will not be to seek rewards, please feel free to give yourself permission to accept them when they come your way. But avoid getting trapped in the recognition game. Some of humility's greatest enemies are soapboxes, microphones and audiences.

The smallest deed is better than the grandest intention. As the saying goes, the road to hell is paved with good intentions. Intention without action is useless, so begin giving service to others regardless of the size of the deed. You will feel better and so will they. It helps to consider service as the rent we pay for the privilege of living on earth.

Giving service to others has many benefits. For example, one university study indicates that regular volunteer work, more than any other activity, dramatically increases life expectancy. It also improves the quality of life because of fewer health problems along the way. Great perks!

Also, another study shows that the majority of all the men and women who have achieved wealth have done it by utilizing their talents and abilities to the maximum in the service of other people. Focusing on others helps us to forget about ourselves. When we do, good things happen and all of our needs are met.

I attend Manresa Retreat House on the banks of the Mississippi River annually for a three-day, silent retreat. Yes, I can be silent on demand! And sometimes Sue demands. Each table in the dining hall seats six retreatants. Many items need to be circulated at the table in order to enjoy the meal. Salt, pepper, coffee, cream, tea, Tabasco Sauce, etc., must find their way to each person in need, all without verbal communication. Each individual focusing on the needs of the others makes this task much easier. While I'm serving the rest, there are five people attending to my needs. A five to one ratio is sizable odds. That is the way it works.

Winston Churchill said, "We make a living by what we get, we make a life by what we give." When simply making a living, we focus on ourselves, while making a life places the emphasis on others. We can not go through life with a catcher's mitt on both hands. That is indicative of only receiving and is one sided. What's needed is balance. Billy Graham was on target when he said, "God has given us two hands — one to receive with and one to give with."

One of the most united acts of service in our community is the annual Cerebral Palsy Telethon on local cable television. This requires literally hundreds of volunteers to pull together for it to be successful. The tasks performed are endless, from emceeing and working cameras to answering telephones and serving food to volunteers. And practically all else in between. This small, bayou community has raised over one million dollars in twenty-two years to help those with Cerebral Palsy. It's a magnificent effort by caring people helping those who are less fortunate. People serve lovingly and give generously.

I have had the pleasure and privilege of serving as an emcee on this live telecast over the years. My partner, Harold, has been a long time friend. The chemistry between us is right as we work in tandem to emcee the show. We banter back and forth unmercifully. I would never dream of doing such a thing if it wasn't for a great cause. Actually, it may well be a repressed desire to be an entertainer. But then that takes talent. Oh, well.

Several years ago, Sue and I were eating at a restaurant nearby. This was a few months after the telethon had aired. There was a couple sitting at a table near us and the man kept staring at me. A few minutes later he snapped his fingers and loudly exclaimed, "Now I know who you are! You're the retarded one on the telethon!" All I could do was laugh. I guess when you put on a clown suit you had better not object to being called Bozo. Service truly does have its rewards!

Opportunities abound for giving service in your community. One can get involved in church, civic organizations, hospitals, schools, professional organizations or virtually any other activity. What is essential is getting involved.

I am a strong advocate of giving service. It feels good, but it also does good. One of the greatest acts of service you can do is to allow yourself to be served. It helps to build up the esteem of others and allows you to affirm yourself. It is indicative of your feelings of worthiness when you allow others to serve you occasionally. It sounds like a win/win situation to me. Adopt the Boys Scouts' motto, "Be Prepared" — to give and to receive.

Attitudinal Affirmation: "I have the mind and heart of a loving servant."

Belief Building Exercise: Make a list of the various ways you could render service to your community and/or profession and in your imagination see yourself in the process of working for each cause. Which one or two create a stir within you? Which make you feel happy, excited, fulfilled and content?

Change Producing Action: Pick one that makes you feel most satisfied and is congruent with your interest and values. Call today to volunteer your services.

T

"You don't have to be good to start, but you have to start to be good."

CHAPTER 20

Talent

"Use what talents you possess. The woods would be very silent if no birds sang except those that sang best."

Unknown

All of us come into the world with talent, special natural ability. It is a gift from God. Although the kind and amount of talent vary among individuals, we have all been blessed with some measure of it.

God's gift to us is more talent and ability than we could ever use in a lifetime. Our gift to God is to develop and utilize as much of that talent and ability as we can. Talent is like a sleeping giant lying dormant within us. It will stay there unless we decide to identify, develop and use it for our good and the welfare of others. It is just sitting there waiting for us to do something with it. A gift must be opened in order to be used.

Not opening them is like going to an Easter egg hunt and not looking for the eggs. They are there but we are not seeking them out. Maybe the reason we have not found our gifts is because we have not been looking with expectancy. Our attitude may be that of, "I wonder if I have any gifts?" This should be changed to "What and where are the gifts I want to develop." This opens us to a state of expectancy which helps to discover those unopened gifts.

In ancient times a talent of silver was worth about $2,000.00.

In the Parable of the Talents found in Matthew's Gospel, the reference is to money and not to actual skill or ability. But the analogy applies to physical talents as well. The parable could be paraphrased as such:

> A Master going on a journey called in his servants and handed his funds over to them according to each man's abilities. To one he disbursed five thousand silver pieces, to a second two thousand, and to a third a thousand. He then went away. Immediately, the man who received the five thousand went to invest it and made another five. In the same way, the man who received two thousand doubled his figure. The man who received the thousand went off instead and dug a hole in the ground, where he buried his master's money. The master was away for a long time. Upon his return he called in his servants to settle accounts. The man who had received five thousand came forward bringing the additional five. "My Lord," he said, "you let me have five thousand. See, I have made five thousand more." His master said to him, "Well done! You are an industrious and reliable servant. Since you were dependable in a small matter I will put you in charge of larger affairs. Come, share your master's joy!" The servant who had received two thousand silver pieces came forward. "My lord," he said, "you entrusted me with two thousand and I have made two thousand more." His master said to him, "Cleverly done! You, too, are an industrious and reliable servant. Since you were dependable in a small matter, I will put you in charge of larger affairs. Come, share your master's joy!" Finally, the man who had received the thousand stepped forward. "My lord," he said, "I knew you were a hard man. You reap where you did not sow and gather where you did not scatter, so out of fear I went off and buried your thousand silver pieces in the ground. Here is your money back." His master exclaimed,

> "You worthless, lazy lout! You know I reap where I did not sow and gather where I did not scatter. All the more reason to deposit my money with the bankers, so that on my return I could have had it back with interest. You, there! Take the thousand away from him and give it to the man with ten thousand. Those who have will get more until they grow rich, while those who have not will lose even the little they have. Throw this worthless servant into the darkness outside, where he can wail and grind his teeth."

The same applies to us. If we ignore our God-given talents, they are not taken from us, but they are wasted as they remain buried deep within. We have been poor stewards. The parable is a good example of wasting our human resources. It is wise to remember that to whom much had been given, much is expected. We will be held accountable.

The parable also reveals that there were varying amounts of talent distributed, but each servant was expected to do something with what he had. The kind and amount is not as important as what is done with it. When we take whatever the Lord has given us and utilize it to the fullest extent, we're showing appreciation for God's gifts. This tends to build-up our self-esteem as well.

Many people have the mistaken notion that if they were talented, their talent would reveal itself in perfect form. In reality, what we are given as human beings is raw talent — the seeds of talent. Just as a plant does not appear fully grown in an instant, the seeds of talent need to be cultivated, developed and nurtured. We don't buy a fiddle today and play in Carnegie Hall tomorrow.

A little league baseball player does not graduate directly to the majors. He improves through various stages of development at different levels. He continuously moves to higher levels as he becomes more proficient, until he reaches the professional ranks. Even here there is room for further growth and improvement.

You don't have to be good to start, but you have to start to be good. It is a lifelong process. Pablo Casals, the great cellist, was asked why, at age eighty-five he continued to practice five hours a day. His reply was, "Because I think I'm getting better." A Welsh Proverb states, "Without perseverance talent is a barren bed." Perseverance, commitment and desire are essential for maximizing our talent. We should keep in mind that the man on top of the mountain didn't fall there.

It is frightening the number of people today who are looking forward to an early retirement in order to quit *doing* and just *being*. They are looking forward to turning off their engine in the prime of their life, wasting the years which could be the most productive of all. Grandma Moses was seventy-eight when she began painting. Michelangelo was seventy-four when he began painting the ceiling of the Sistine Chapel and was still working on it at his death at age eighty-four. The use it or lose it principle applies. Age has absolutely nothing to do with talent, except providing the opportunity to be used more.

I have been a bit too serious in this chapter thus far. Perhaps it is time for a shift. Note that talent is not always easily recognizable. A man seeking work walked into an employment agency. The clerk asked, "What kind of work do you do?" "I do bird imitations," said the man. The clerk replied, "I'm sorry but we don't have a need for that sort of thing." At this point the man stood up, began flapping his arms and flew out of the office. Look deeply when seeking to discover hidden talent in yourself and others. Discovery means finding something that's already there, so look closely since the talent may not be very obvious.

According to Erica Jong, "Everyone has talent. What is rare is the courage to follow the talent to the dark places where it leads." It means leaving our comfort zone and taking risks. Remember, too, that people perform at their best when contributing their talents to something in which they believe. So look around and see what peaks your interest. Your interest will lead to your talent which will help you to make a difference in the world.

One of the most remarkable displays of talent I have ever seen was at the last two NSA (National Speakers Association) Conventions. It was in the person of Ken Medema. Ken is blind and incredibly gifted. As the general session speaker gave his/her presentation, Ken sat in the front row in the audience and listened. At the end of the talk, he was immediately led on stage and seated at a piano. He then played and sang an original composition containing all of the major points in the talk just given. Ken had composed this in his head as he listened. It is very powerful to witness something like this. Without question, this magnificent gift can only come from God. I get "frissons" (oops, pardon my Cajun, goose bumps) just talking about it! The battle cry now at the convention is, "The convention doesn't start until the blind man sings!"

We may not have talent as extraordinary as Ken's, but what we do have is incumbent upon us to use. And we do not need to be experts either. An expert does not necessarily know more than you, he just has it better organized and uses slides.

I don't want to reach the Pearly Gates and have the Lord say to me, "Get out of my sight you worthless, lazy lout! I gave you an abundance of talent and ability and you buried it!" No, I want Him to say, "Well done, Curt! You were an industrious and reliable servant! Come, share your Master's joy."

Attitudinal Affirmation: "I am blessed with an abundance of talent and I use it for others every day."

Belief Building Exercise: Make a list of your talents. Ask a close friend or family member to review your list to see if more can be added. We oftentimes short-change ourselves.

Change Producing Action: Select one of your budding talents or interests. Decide on a course of action to develop it and then use it in the service of others.

THOUGHTS & ACTION STEPS

U

"An empathetic listener listens with the heart as well as the ears."

CHAPTER 21

UNDERSTANDING

"O Divine Master, grant that I may not so much seek to be consoled as to console, to be understood as to understand."

PRAYER OF ST. FRANCIS

When I first wrote this chapter, my book buddy, Tina Thomas, said it was funny but she didn't know what my point was. I jumped from understanding in listening, to understanding the meaning of life, to understanding what upsets us in others, to understanding that I really did not quite understand what I wanted to say myself. Understand?

After re-reading, it became clear to me that the message I want to convey is that while we all want to be understood, understanding another is many times more valuable to the relationship and ultimately the most elegant, loving and efficient way of meeting our need to be understood.

Understanding can be likened to two people vying for a meal with the illusion that only one course exists. They will both be grasping for the food with little or no regard for each other and for what else is to come. They have lost focus and both will lose out.

Understanding is the key to fruitful relationships. It is being sympathetic, considerate and accepting. It is coming to know the other person's point of view – wrapped in all of his hopes, dreams, joys, sorrow and pain. Then and only then can we know why he responds to us in the manner in which he does.

Most frequently, however, we are self-absorbed and want to be understood rather than make the attempt to understand. If both people are talking, then no one is listening. Is it any wonder that there are problems. Focusing attention on the other person indicates our care and concern for him and provides much needed insight necessary for good communication.

"Seek first to understand then to be understood" is Habit #5 in Stephen Covey's 7 Habits. There is a need to reach out to others in order to be effective. One of the successful ways is to be an intense listener. By so doing we can become more empathic with the other person and their situation. It allows us to empathize which enables us to sympathize.

Active listening is a method of validating or confirming understanding. For example, Tom makes a statement. Mary reiterates the statement in her own words. If Tom agrees that Mary has already understood, then Mary makes a response. Mary now makes a statement, and Tom states the message she wants to convey. It is like a volleyball game, but before hitting the ball back over the net, the receiver must fully describe what the sender means.

Being a good listener doesn't mean you agree with the person; it simply means you are trying to understand him. An empathic listener listens with the heart as well as the ears. He hears emotions and feelings as well as words. Sue has told me on a number of occasions that I have a speech impediment — I don't listen! There is some truth to that. I am aware that listening is my weakest communication skill and is in need of improvement. And don't for a second think she doesn't remind me of it — often!

Effective communication requires that the speaker and listener be on the same frequency. If they are not, there will be a lack of understanding. For instance, coming home from school one day, I found my eight year old niece, Tiva, sitting on the steps. She was playing with a make-up kit and had put on lavish amount of powder, rouge and lipstick. I leaned over and kissed her. Realizing that I had gotten some of the make-up on me, I told her, "I had better wipe this stuff off my face. What would nanny (Sue) think if she came home and found lipstick on Cu-Curt?" Tiva replied, "Huhhh, nanny would think you'd been playing in her make-up kit!"

Dale Carnegie, in his book How To Win Friends And Influence People, says that the best way to have people like you is to genuinely listen to them. This provides a sense of importance and boosts their self-esteem. They in turn will reciprocate. When you can, avoid focusing on yourself and your interests. To do so is egotistical. An egotist can be described as someone who is "me-deep" in conversation. It is like the guy who babbled on for half an hour about himself and then said to the other person, "Let's talk about you for awhile. Tell me what *you* like most about me."

Listening to others with our heart is helpful in maintaining and nourishing our relationship with those we love. Also listening to ourselves with our heart will nourish us and encourage growth. When we open our heart in an effort to understand our (heart's) desires, we can seek out those people, situations and circumstances which nourish us. Also, by listening to our heart's discontent, such as when we feel aggravated or uncomfortable around someone, we can better understand ourselves.

According to Carl Jung, "Everything that irritates us about others can lead us to a better understanding of ourselves." The reason we dislike certain habits and characteristics in others is because we dislike them in ourselves. We possess the same habits but do not want to admit it; therefore, we transfer that dislike to others. Be observant and note if this holds true for you. You may be surprised. When you look for the good in others, you will discover the best in yourself.

What we do not understand generally tends to frighten us, like the aging process for example. People dread growing old. But considering the alternative isn't that great, it would do us a lot of good to work at understanding this process. For instance, all of the mystique surrounding turning thirty. Choooo! (Oops, there goes my Cajun again!) It's so simple. Thirty is that magical age when we stop listening to the Stones and start passing them. Nothing tough to understand about that.

Understanding means only to comprehend or to relate. Notice it does not mean agree with, accept or judge. To understand someone calls for the capacity to put ourselves aside and relate to someone else's viewpoint and feelings given their values, limits and circumstances.

A bit of sage advice that supports this perspective is, "Never try to teach a pig to sing. It will only frustrate you and annoy the pig." Once we understand that pigs do not sing, we do not judge that they should and waste our energy or emotion trying to convince them to go against their nature.

Sometimes understanding doesn't happen immediately. It takes an openness to inspiration to understand some people or events over time. For instance, a survey shows that professional wrestling on television is taken seriously by ninety-three percent of the viewers. That's disturbing when you consider that some of them are registered voters. After years of confusion, I now understand how some of those politicians got into office!

Understanding ourselves and others is essential for successful, loving relationships. Being kind, generous and thoughtful can help to ensure positive interaction and provide the necessary nurturing. Understanding is a two-way street; therefore, put forth your share of the effort. People who understand each other provide mutual support and encouragement which in turn builds self-esteem. Seek first to understand.

Attitudinal Affirmation: "I do my best to understand the people in my life."

Belief Building Exercise: Recall the last disagreement you had with your spouse or significant other. Identify what caused the problem. Decide how you could have been more compassionate, caring and understanding.

Change Producing Action: In all your conversations tomorrow, focus on the other person. Keep the conversation totally centered on them and away from you. Listen with your heart as well as your ears. See if you feel differently.

V

"Whatever you intensely visualize, strongly desire, sincerely believe and enthusiastically act upon will surely become a reality."

CHAPTER 22

Visualization

"Losers visualize the penalties of failure. Winners visualize the rewards of success."

Dr. Rob Gilbert

Visualization is the positive use of the imagination. To visualize is to see what is not there. It is creating a mental picture of how you want to be or what you want to become. Everyone's life is a record of his or her visualization, or lack of it. It is how we draw our own roadmaps and create our own lives.

How you visualize yourself determines who you are. Every seed contains the master plan of what that seed is supposed to become. An acorn, for example, has all the ingredients necessary to become an oak tree. Proper nourishment and time are all that is needed. We are no different. Once we plant the seed in our mind of what we want to become, then time, effort and nourishment will bring that vision to reality.

We look at a huge block of granite and see nothing but a large stone. Yet, a sculptor looks at that same block of granite and sees a magnificent statue in it. Using a hammer and chisel, he fashions a life-size statue from the hard mass. The statue was actually created the moment the sculptor visualized it in his mind. That is when it took form and shape and became as real as the finished product. We are creators and created in our mind as well.

We should carry in our mind a picture of what we want to be. We decide what it is we want, then picture ourselves as having already attained it. Whatever we intensely visualize, strongly desire, sincerely believe and enthusiastically act upon will surely become a reality. Those who can see the invisible can do the impossible.

Visualization or imaging is mental simulation. Actually, we are pretending to be or do something in order to give specific directions to the subconscious mind. Since the subconscious mind can not distinguish between a real experience and a vividly imagined one, the simulation appears real and the mind works diligently to make it become a reality. The key to the most effective visualization is to utilize as many of the senses as possible.

A demonstration was performed some years ago by a hypnotist. His subject was hypnotized and told that he was going to be touched on his arm with a red hot poker. In reality, he was touched very lightly with an ordinary lead pencil. In just a few moments his arm turned red and shortly thereafter, a blister formed on his skin. The subconscious mind is very powerful and does what it is programmed to do.

Dr. Charles Garfield has done extensive research on peak performers, both in athletics and in business. One of the main findings of his research is that almost all world-class athletes and other peak performers are visualizers. The action is created in the mind before it is performed by the body.

We have all witnessed athletes in deep concentration on the physical task at hand. It might be shooting a free throw in basketball, putting in golf or preparing to release the ball in bowling. Standing very still, they appear to be staring into space but, in essence, are visualizing. They are "seeing" the action that they want being performed in their mind and preparing the body to follow suit.

We can program ourselves in exactly the same way in our everyday lives. I use visualization in preparing for speeches. I usually know the type of room, its physical arrangement and the number of people attending. I also know what suit and tie I am going to wear. Hey, I'm psychic! I see myself presenting to the group and since I use a lot of humor, I picture the attendees laughing. They continually nod their head in affirmation and applaud when I finish. Everything goes according to plan and the presentation is successful! Crazy? No! I am simply setting myself up for success. And why shouldn't I? It's my vision! Why would I want to visualize failure?

In an example I related earlier, Sue used visualization along with the affirmation tape in her quest to bowl a 600 scratch series. Upon returning home one Tuesday evening, I asked her how she had done. She said, "Great, but I'm exhausted!" "Why?" I asked. She answered," Well, as I got in position, I saw myself releasing the ball. In my mind I watched it go all the way down the alley and knock down every pin. Strike! Then I actually bowled." I again asked, "So what's exhausting?" She replied, "After bowling three games in my mind and three on the alley, I'm burned out!"

Visualization is associated with the right side of the brain. That is where the creative, imaginative part is housed. The left side produces the sequential, structured type, like me. Ideally, both sides of the brain should be used in order to achieve balance. I was using both sides of the brain and thought I was doing O.K. Then I found out that I was using back and front instead of left and right. That's a "no brainer." No wonder I was confused!

There are some people who have difficulty visualizing. This may be partially due to not knowing how, but for many it is not really believing they can achieve their desired dream or goal. They are boxed in by a psychological ceiling and walls which prevent their mind from expanding and creating. I believe this situation stems from low self-esteem. They don't believe they are worthy of having what they really want and can not imagine themselves having it.

Here is a simple procedure for using the visualization tool. First, find a quiet, peaceful place. Now get into a comfortable position and relax. Just let yourself go. Close your eyes and breathe slowly. Inhale through the nose and exhale through your mouth. Clearly picture in your mind the way you want to be. Hold that image. Listen to the sounds. Notice all the colors involved. Accentuate the positive and believe. Allow this image to be imbedded in your mind. Do this as often as you like but especially before going to sleep at night. Your subconscious mind will work feverishly to make it become a reality.

The philosopher Goethe said, "Whatever you do or dream you can do, begin it. Boldness has genius, power and magic in it." Begin now to visualize yourself as a winner. See yourself as a kind, loving, capable, successful person, and your self-esteem will improve immeasurably. I can "see" it happening!

Attitudinal Affirmation: "I see myself becoming the person I want to be."

Belief Building Exercise: Make a list of the qualities that would strengthen your self-esteem. Decide how these would affect your appearance and behavior and develop a mental picture of this. Play this picture in your mind as if it were so.

C**hange Producing Action:** Use the visualization procedure described in this chapter two to three times daily to make your new mental picture become a reality.

W

"Realizing our self-worth helps us to realize our dreams."

CHAPTER 23

Worth

"So much is a man worth as he esteems himself"
Francois Rabelais

Worth is a feeling of deserving or of importance. Self-worth means that we recognize our value and appreciate ourselves. Feelings of worthiness are critical for our emotional and psychological health and well-being.

You and I have tremendous worth because we were made in the image of God. And God don't make no junk! To be created in God's image means that we are a reflection or an imprint of Him. We have worth by virtue of the fact that we are His creation. I remember a parent coming to school for a conference to discuss her son's behavior problems. In the course of conversation, she said, "I don't love him because he is good, I love him because he is mine."

For many of us that sense of worth began to erode as we grew up. Well meaning parents and loved ones inadvertently cracked the protective armor and began the slow process of deteriorating our self-worth. Continuously being told no, stop, don't, mustn't, shouldn't, etc. led us to believe that we were not good enough. One psychologist has estimated that the average eighteen-year-old has been told no or what he could not do 148,000 times since birth. This, coupled with phrases like "You're lazy," "You'll never amount to anything," and "You never do anything right," provided such a devastating blow to our self-worth that some were never able to recover from it. For many it was a knock-out punch. Is it any wonder?

It is important to recognize and appreciate our worth as well as the worth of others. It will have a dramatic impact on our interactions every day. Know that worth has to do with *being*, not doing. You have worth because of who you are, not for what you do. Worth has nothing to do with beauty, talent, money, position or any other criterion. It has to do with *you*, period. Marrying someone for their looks is similar to buying a house for the paint. What matters most is what is on the inside and that is where worth resides.

Some people tend to put others down in an attempt to build up their own self-worth. To belittle is to "be little." Gossiping or talking negatively about your neighbor will no more increase your worth than taking a sledge hammer and smashing your neighbor's car will make your car look better.

Accepting our worth as a person will prevent us from playing the comparison game. We run into problems when we start measuring ourselves against others. There is no need to simply because there is no standard, except Jesus Christ, and we all fall short there.

We become attracted to titles, positions, clothes and other material things that many in society have come to associate with worth. These are superficial and actually have very little meaning. I have seen this demonstrated repeatedly with my work in the Kairos Prison Ministry.

I never cease to be amazed at the caliber of individuals who volunteer for this ministry. On any given Kairos team, one can routinely find engineers, lawyers, physical therapists, an IRS agent, an Assistant U.S. Attorney and many others. One was even a candidate for Governor of Louisiana. The point is that when all come together for team meetings dressed in casual clothes, there are no visible distinctions. All are brothers in Christ, ready to serve. Titles are left at home. All have equal worth and value and are ready to contribute.

On Friday of a Kairos weekend, a group picture is taken of the inmates and the team. A copy is given to everyone participating. A friend of mine was looking at the picture a few weeks later. He pointed to one and asked, "Is this a prisoner?" "No," I said, "That's a priest." He pointed to another and asked, " Is this one a prisoner?" "No," I replied. "That's a lawyer. He could be, though!" Just kidding! My friend could not tell the players without a scorecard, and neither can we. Shedding all superficiality puts us on an even keel. Worth is inherent within us and is not determined by outside factors.

This little tidbit is just too good to pass up, so I will share it with you. The IRS agent and I began working Kairos together more than three years ago. Clint and I have become good friends during that time. On one occasion, as we were waiting outside the front gates of Angola to be cleared for admittance, I spotted a bumper sticker on a car in the parking lot. It read, "Help stamp out organized crime. Abolish the IRS!" Needless to say I created havoc for Clint on the weekend by "accidentally" bringing it out in my talk to the inmates. As fate would have it, the focus for the weekend retreat was on Zacchaeus, the much despised tax collector. Clint became "Zack" for the weekend and maybe forever.

One aspect of the Power of Positive Students Program that we implemented at Golden Meadow Middle School was to post positive signs and slogans around campus. This was utilizing visual conditioning to intentionally place a message into the subconscious mind. Over the doorway going to the cafeteria was the sign, "I'm worth it!" Too many kids were not receiving this message on a regular basis. This method ensured that they were exposed to it everyday. When we do our best to affirm others daily about their worth, we affirm our worth as well.

Realizing our self-worth helps us to realize our dreams. When we know our dream, know that we are worthy of that dream. We program that sense of worthiness into every fiber of our being. Thoreau said, "People were born to succeed, not fail." But much depends upon whether or not we think we are worth it.

Although we understand and accept our worth, we ought not take ourselves too seriously. A Chinese Proverb states, "Blessed is he who can laugh at himself. He shall never cease to be entertained." We do some goofy things at times and benefit by seeing the humor in it.

A classic example was the time my "book buddy", Tina, and I were reviewing each other's manuscript. Taking a break, we drove to McDonald's to get a soft drink. Engrossed in conversation, I inadvertently passed up the drive-up window and came to a stop at the Sunday newspaper stand – and waited for the voice through the speaker to take my order. With a hearty laugh Tina said jokingly, "You don't come here very often, do you?" In a semi-state of embarrassment, I backed up slowly to the "real" window. It was funny even though it was at my expense.

We should learn to value and appreciate ourselves in spite of what goes on around us. When we do, we recognize our worth which is the cornerstone for building self-esteem. What really matters is what happens in us, not to us. Let it happen *in* you!

Attitudinal Affirmation: " I am worthy of succeeding at anything I do."

Belief Building Exercise: Write on a sheet of paper all the reasons you know you have worth. Do the same for those closest to you.

Change Producing Action: Share with family and friends your ideas about your worth. Also share how you see worth in them.

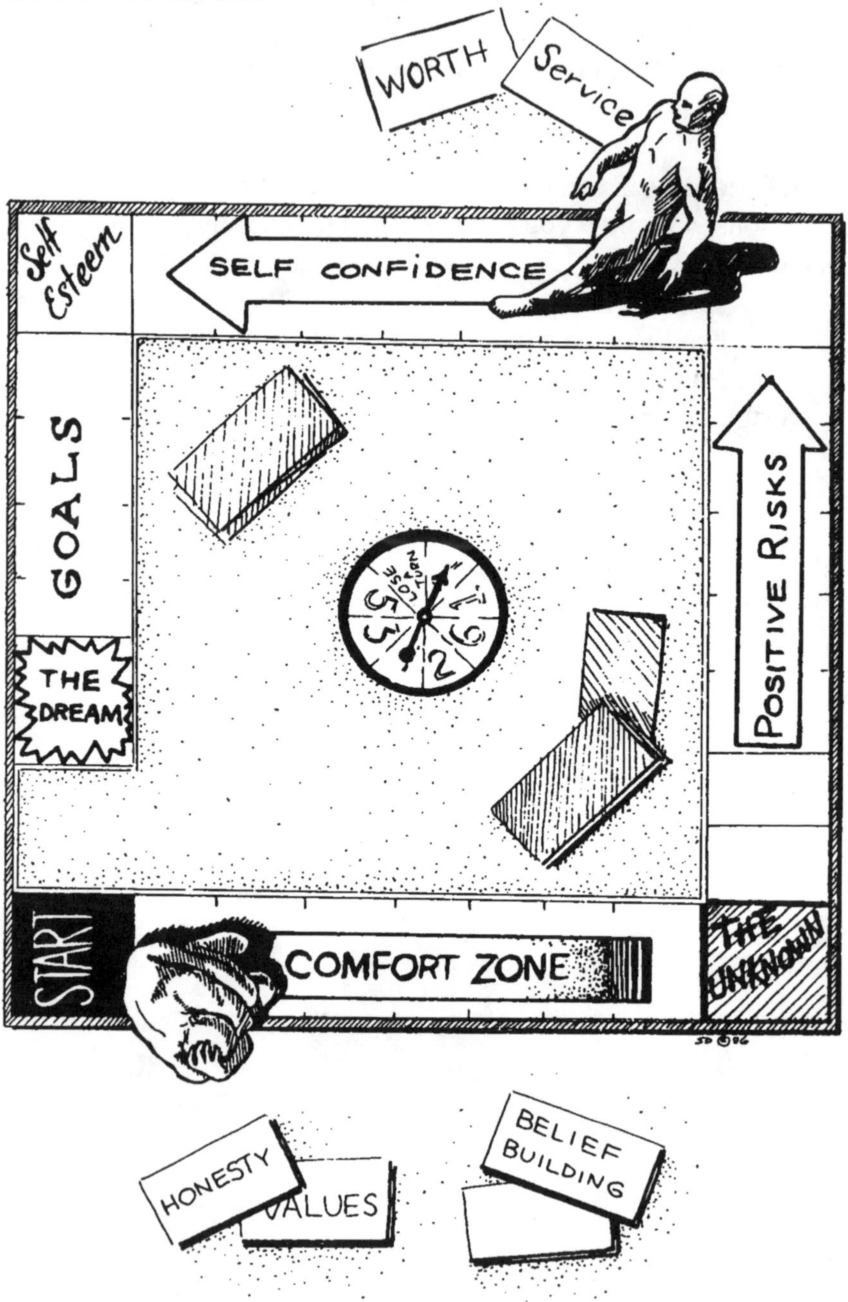

"Self-Esteem makes the game of life 'Worth It!'"

THOUGHTS & ACTION STEPS

X

"Life is a self-fulfilling prophecy. We don't always get what we want, but usually get what we expect."

CHAPTER 24

XPECTATIONS

"That which you fear or expect most will surely come to pass. The body manifests what the mind harbors."
PROVERB

"I'm hoping for the best but expecting the worst." What a doomsday philosophy! Yet, that is the way many people approach life. They do not realize that life is a self-fulfilling prophecy. We don't always get what we want, but usually get what we expect.

Expectation is nothing more than the mental attitude of anticipation. When we expect a certain thing to happen, the subconscious mind immediately sets out to make it become a reality regardless of whether it is good or bad. Isaac Singer said, "If you keep on saying things are going to be bad, you have a good chance of being a prophet." So true. The first grader was talking about the recent fire in his school. "I knew it was going to happen," he said, "we've been practicing for it all year!"

We perform to the lowest level of our expectations. And so do others. Expect a little and you get a little; expect a lot and you will probably get a lot. As a principal, I gave this message every year to my faculty on orientation day: "I expect a lot from you but I want you to expect a lot from me. *I* expect a lot from me." I wanted them to know that it was a two way street. Julius Irving, the former all-pro basketball player, said, "I demand more from myself than anyone else could ever expect." When you live by that kind of philosophy you will never short-change anybody, including yourself.

Determine to focus on the good with high expectations. Be aware of your thoughts because they inevitably become reality. Like Job, "That which I greatly fear has come upon me." Positive thoughts ensure that only good will come upon you. As one sign said, "We are realists here. We expect a miracle every day."

We need to be careful about creating unrealistic expectations. When expectations are too high and not realistic, we invite frustration. The doctor was finishing putting a cast on the broken arm of a patient. The patient asked, "Doctor, will I be able to play the piano once my arm heals?" The doctor answered, "Of course!" The patient replied, "That's strange." "Why?" asked the doctor. "Because I couldn't play it before I broke my arm!" said the patient.

Keep your expectations of others in perspective and reasonable. Many parents today want their children to have things they did not have, like straight A's on report cards. If the potential is there, then it is O.K. The expectation should be equal to the ability or what the person can reasonably deliver.

Sometimes our expectations can give us peace of mind or be a source of concern. I was boarding a U.S. Air flight headed for the east coast. Two weeks earlier one of their planes had crashed in New York because of over-shooting the runway. The pilot pushed the wrong lever.

It was a Sunday morning and the flight was packed, so boarding was very slow. I guess all these folks were counting on the law of averages; nothing could possibly happen this quickly again, right? That, however, was not my logic. I had booked that flight a month earlier and was not eager to pay penalties for a change. Standing outside the plane in the chute, I was able to see into the cockpit. There, to my surprise, was the pilot with feet propped up nonchalantly looking at the comic strip. I said to the flight attendant, "In light of what happened with Flight 286 in New York two weeks ago, I expect the pilot to be doing something just a little bit more constructive than reading Beetle Bailey — like reviewing the flight plan, checking the instrument panel or reading Flying 101!" Peace of mind or source of concern? You decide.

Expectations can have an enormous effect on our health. Studies repeatedly indicate that negative thinking and expectations can bring on illness and disease. Norman Cousins in his book, Anatomy of An Illness, states that seventy-five percent of our illnesses are self induced. They are psychosomatic. We become sick because we believe we are going to be sick. Remember the discussion on the power of the subconscious mind? It is within our realm of control.

On the positive side, the mind can help us to become healthy again. Placebos are fake medicines with absolutely no medicinal value whatsoever. Yet, when taken, believing they are the "real thing", produce relief from pain and bring healing. The basic ingredients are expectations and belief. Food for thought, don't you think? And speaking of food, this reminds me of an incident occurring at a food concession at the Atlanta airport. Airports are notorious for their high prices. I was in line behind a family of four. When the clerk rang up all the items and gave the father the total, he exclaimed, "Good God! I expected to spend a lot of money on my vacation, but not at the airport!" Good point, but things don't always measure up to our expectations.

Be cautious when expecting something from someone in public. It is wise to check with that person beforehand in order to avoid embarrassment. I was presiding at a Lions Club Officer Installation Banquet several years ago. Wives and guests were present for the occasion and attendance was quite good. Meetings customarily begin with the Pledge to the Flag and the Blessing. One member led us in the Pledge, and then I called on Lion Pat to say the Blessing without giving him prior notice.

Pat cleared his throat. Then a second time. A third. Again. And again. At this point I realized that he did not know it. (the standard one) After what appeared to be an eternity, I quickly began to lead the group in the Blessing. After the program I apologized to Pat for what had happened. I told him, "It never dawned on me that you might not know it. After all, you are a good Christian and are active in the church." He responded, "Yes, but I don't eat in church!" That taught me a good lesson about expectations that I shall always remember. Take very little for granted.

Having high expectations means we expect good to happen. It is an indication that our self-esteem is up, too. We believe that good should happen to us and for us and are deserving. When it does, we are deeply grateful. Always expect the best — for yourself and others!

Attitudinal Affirmation: "I expect the best for myself because I deserve it."

Belief Building Exercise: Review the situations which were most important to you last week. How did each one turn out? What were your expectations going into each situation? Did the outcomes match your expectations?

Change Producing Action: Determine your most important situation in the coming week. Think positive thoughts about the outcome and have high expectations. Visualize great results, too.

Y

"Yesterday's dreams are the realities of tomorrow when they become today's desire."

CHAPTER 25

YEARNING

"Success requires heart and soul effort and you can only put heart and soul into something you really desire."

DAVID SCHWARTZ, PH.D.

To yearn is to desire earnestly. It is a deep hunger within to have, to be or to do. It is so strong you can almost feel the ache in your body. Yearning is a burning passion which lights a fire in your soul.

We may yearn for fame, fortune, happiness, success or a multitude of other things. To yearn for something indicates some measure of dissatisfaction with what you have or what you are. I have heard this referred to as inspirational dissatisfaction. You want more and that is all right because desire is where achievement begins. Capable people fail without desire, and with it, underdogs win. If you were completely satisfied, you would not be desiring more or something different.

While still a principal, I had the opportunity to deliver a keynote at a conference in Williamsburg, Virginia. It was challenging and filled me with a freedom I had not felt before. I was able to visit Colonial Williamsburg and other places of interest while there. That weekend experience opened my eyes and heart to many things. It has been said that "A taste of honey is worse than none at all." Well, I had tasted the honey and I wanted more. There was no keeping the kid down on the farm now!

A yearning burned deep inside of me to pursue a career in speaking. I knew this was what I wanted to do with my life and six and one-half years seemed like an eternity to wait for the thirty-year teacher retirement. The Lord intervened and helped me to make the decision. It caught everyone by surprise because this was so uncharacteristic of me. Remember me, left brain — logical, ordered, sequential, calculating?

I can truthfully say that this was the hardest decision I ever made, and, yet, it was the easiest decision I have ever made. What a paradox! But that is what happens when you find your purpose and become passionate about it. That yearning inside says, "Let go of the security and safety and go for it!"

The last thing I wanted was to reach age sixty-five or so and say, "Gosh, I wish I would have had the courage to take a risk and follow my dreams when I was forty-five." I did not want to say, "I wish I would have done this or I wish I would have done that," or, "I should have done this or I should have done that." No, I did not want to "should on" myself nor have any regret.

It is impossible to describe the experiences that I have had these last seven years as a speaker. The people that I have met, places I have been and things I have been able to do are incredible. In many respects, I am a different person because of the personal and professional growth that has taken place. I would not trade this for anything in the world, but I would not trade my twenty-four years in education, either. I believe the two complement each other and were necessary for me to be where I am in my life today.

Change is good and oftentimes needed. Yet, it is important to remember to be thankful for what we have while we are on our way to having more. It is equally important to be thankful for who we are while we are on our way to becoming more.

Gratitude expresses appreciation for the moment while in the process of becoming and doing more. Listening closely to the yearning within will lead us to where we should go or what we should do.

It is reasonable to say that your dreams create the inner yearning. People who act on their dreams are winners. It is easy to tell winners from losers. Winners always watch for an opportunity and losers always squander every opportunity. What are your dreams, desires, passions, yearnings?

Strong desire gives birth to great accomplishment. Be determined to succeed. Desire to win. Then, if you act upon your dreams, nothing is beyond your grasp. But you must want it badly.

The story is told of the wise old sage who lived on the side of a mountain near a lake. One day a young man came to him and said, "I am told that you can give me the secret of success in life." The sage stood up and led the young man to the lake. He then asked the young man to place his head under the water. The sage placed both his hands on the submerged head and held it there until the young man summoned every ounce of his strength to break the grasp and pull his head from the water. As the young man sat gasping for breath, the sage told him, "Young man, when you want success as much as you wanted that breath of air, you will have found the secret." Success can be as sustaining as life itself. But just yearning and desiring are not enough. We have to work for it. Never itch for anything you are not willing to scratch for.

Yearn for your dreams and the yearning will cause you to act on your dreams. Yesterday's dreams are the reality of tomorrow when they become today's desires. That was the case with writing this book. It was a part of my dream when I left the school system. In spite of being self-disciplined and committed, starting the book always seemed secondary to all else. It was not until recently that this yearning was set into motion.

It all started innocently enough at the NSA Workshop in St. Louis. Fellow NSAer Tina Thomas asked the seemingly harmless question, "Curt, when are you going to write a book?" My response was the usual, "Soon." Not accepting this as an answer, she pinned me down to agreeing to complete it in six months. And then she had the audacity to hold me to that commitment! She wanted to write a book, too, so she suggested we work together to help, support and encourage each other. That is how we became "book buddies."

Several weeks into the writing process, we met at Tina's home to review the chapters completed thus far. She then convinced me to knock two months off of the original six month time frame. My hypoglycemia must have reacted to cause some light-headedness. Had I been in total control of my faculties, I would have never agreed. However, meeting on a weekly basis enhanced my yearning and prompted me to finish the manuscript in three months, three weeks ahead of schedule. The more I saw the book taking shape and substance, the more I yearned to see it completed and in print. For Tina's unrelenting persistence in keeping me on task, I have affectionately nicknamed her Simon Legree after the infamous slave owner. My point is that desire or yearning coupled with action produces results. And if it takes someone to prod you along, so be it.

If you yearn to improve your self-esteem, an excellent starting point would be to faithfully use the affirmations, exercises and actions at the end of each chapter. Knowing you need to improve your self-esteem and knowing how to do it is not enough. There must be a desire to do it. Distance runner Jim Ryun said, "Motivation gets you started, habit keeps you going." Let the yearning within be the catalyst to jump-start you. Then let the habit drive the process. Your self-esteem will be enhanced as you stick with it and become the kind of person you yearn to be.

Attitudinal Affirmation: "I yearn for things that make me a better person."

Belief Building Exercise: Make a list of the things you truly desire. Prioritize your list according to how passionate you are about each one and the ones which are most realistic to achieve.

Change Producing Action: Take your number one yearning or desire and set it up as a goal. Use the goal-setting process described in chapter seven to make it become a reality.

Z

"Having zeal and passion in our lives can be the spice that makes the difference."

CHAPTER 26

Zeal

> *"Let everything you do be done as if it makes a difference."*
>
> William James

Zeal is defined as eager desire or effort. It is a state of being filled with passion, spirit and determination. An English proverb describes zeal as "fire without light." This fire prompts us to look forward to each new day with eagerness and enthusiasm.

Being zealous creates excitement about life and living. It is living life to the fullest by giving totally of self. Zeal helps us to be proactive. We do not sit around letting life live us; we make things happen. Approaching a situation with zeal is indicative of the confidence in our ability to handle it effectively. This confidence in turn helps to build our self-esteem.

The pressures of modern day living place a considerable amount of stress on families. Stress can bring on difficult times. A lack of zeal can cause us to want to withdraw when life becomes difficult. The trouble with many of us is that in trying times, we stop trying. But a person with zeal has determination and never yields. He continues to search for viable solutions to problems and challenges which will produce successful outcomes. The words "quit" and "defeat" are not in his vocabulary.

Zeal is also vital in our chosen work since we spend much

time on the job. If excitement is not inherent in our work, then it is our responsibility to bring excitement to it. How we approach our vocation makes the difference. When we envision our work as dull and boring, we are inviting misery. I touched on this in chapter ten on "Joy."

We have the choice of bringing enthusiasm to our work, or finding new employment. But to remain in a job just going through the motions for a paycheck is courting disaster. It is not fair to us nor to our employers.

I enjoyed my ten years as principal of Golden Meadow Middle School, but to say that every aspect of it was enjoyable would not be truthful. What I did not like was what I refer to as the m & m of the job, the minutia and manure, which destroys zeal. These are the insignificant, the expendable, yet must be confronted. And when you deal with so many people, there will be much that is unpleasant. Nevertheless, I did attempt to approach my work with zeal and enthusiasm. And for the most part, I believe I succeeded.

One of the most zealous incidents and one I have shared in many of my talks is what I call the "Gorilla Story." In October of my first year as principal, two parents' club officers came to see me to discuss an upcoming student activity. They related that it was customary for the parents to put on a haunted house for the kids on Halloween and were seeking permission to do so again. I agreed. They asked if I wanted to participate. I said yes, but did not have a costume. They assured me they would provide one.

On that fateful Halloween Day, the two ladies presented me with a large, brown paper bag. Neatly stacked inside were a pair of coveralls, a white sweatshirt, a gorilla mask and hairy hands and arms extending to the elbow. No one knew about this costume and my participation except these two ladies who vowed secrecy. Putting on the costume, I peeked around the corner into the secretary's office where Peggy was busy at work. I snarled and, seeing only the gorilla head, she screamed. Yessss! I knew I was into something too creative to pass up. So I ran outside, crawled along the building and peeked through the window into the first classroom. The teacher was quite startled and the kids went wild! This was the reaction I was getting from each classroom. Great! I was having a blast..... and then I reached Mrs. Brown's room! (name has been changed to protect the innocent) She is a very fine lady, sophisticated and began her teaching career the year I was born. Always immaculately dressed, she was still neat and well groomed at the end of the day. I suppose you could say, too, that she had a no-nonsense attitude.

I began my gorilla routine by snarling at the window. She looked at me askance and continued teaching. I was being ignored and didn't like it one bit. How dare she! Then I began waving my arms through the window in addition to snarling and making what I thought were plausible gorilla sounds. The result was the same. She just looked at me stiff-necked and stared. Oh Oh! Aw, what the heck. Go for it boy! So I threw one leg across the window creating the appearance of jumping into the room. Apparently, that was the last straw.

Mrs. Brown said, "Bobby, would you go to the office and get Mr. Boudreaux!" Bobby looked up and said meekly, "Uh, uh, Mrs. Brown, uh, uh, I believe that *is* Mr. Boudreaux." Mrs. Brown replied, "Don't be ridiculous! Mr. Boudreaux wouldn't stoop to doing something so low!" At which time I began whimpering and slowly meandering away. I know when to cut my losses and move on. Needless to say, Mrs. Brown was surprised when she learned at recess that it was really me. That was the prettiest shade of red I had seen in a long time.

Sometimes, though, I can take my zeal a little too far. One night I put the gorilla mask on when going to bed and pulled the covers over my head. Sue came to kiss me good night. Upon pulling the covers back and seeing the gorilla (I'm not sure which one), she screamed frantically and began crying. She admonished, "If you ever do that to me again, I'll leave you!" There's just no end to her sense of humor! But it is good to know I have options! By the way, the gorilla outfit is tucked away close at hand in my office closet if ever I should need it.

We need zeal in all facets of our lives, but especially in our family and work. When we relate to family members with excitement and enthusiasm, we clearly show how we enjoy being with them and their significance to us. They will respond in kind which strengthens the relationship. We are delighted to be in the company of enthusiastic, spirited and passionate people because they tend to rub off on us.

A husband came home and told his wife, "Honey, I found a great job today! Good salary, paid holidays, free health insurance and four weeks vacation." "Wow!" That's wonderful dear," replied his wife. To which he added, "I knew you'd be pleased. By the way, you start Monday!" Just be careful not to be over zealous, the consequences could be staggering.

I approach my career in speaking with zeal and passion. It is what I want to do as long as I can walk and talk. Although it is work, it is very enjoyable. Writing is work, too, but I derive a certain satisfaction from it. I hope I have been able to convey that message to you throughout the pages of this book.

Having zeal and passion in our lives can be the spice that makes the difference. It is up to us. Being excited about life and living creates excitement in ourselves. That excitement helps to enhance our self-esteem. The higher our self-esteem, the more zeal we will have for life. Put a little spice in your life!

Attitudinal Affirmation: "I approach life and living with zest and zeal."

Belief Building Exercise: Examine yesterday's activities. Take note of the one(s) you addressed without zeal. Determine why you were not enthusiastic. Identify the major tasks facing you tomorrow and make a list.

Change Producing Action: From the list, take the task you least like to do and commit to doing it first with zeal and passion. See how you feel about the task after completing it.

"Self-esteem is crucial for living a quality life and having a positive impact on society."

SUMMARY

"I regard self-esteem as the single most powerful force in our existence. The way we feel about ourselves affects virtually every aspect of our lives."

Dr. Nathaniel Branden

One of the most deeply rooted and compelling motivations we have is the need to like ourselves. Self-esteem is crucial for living a quality life and having a positive impact on society. But as was explained in the introduction, it is our individual choice.

A study of five thousand people a few years ago revealed that at least three out of four did not have high self-esteem. That is an eye-opening figure and indicative of how prevalent the problem of low self-esteem is in society. In light of this, I believe it is incumbent upon each one of us to continuously improve our self-esteem and help others do the same. That is making a worthwhile contribution to the improvement of society.

I believe each one of us has been chosen by God to do some work no other person on this earth can do. That is our purpose. Seek to find your purpose and begin to accomplish it. Doing so will give more meaning and value to your life and help you to feel better about yourself. The higher your self-esteem, the more you can be "on purpose" and able to fulfill God's plan.

Following the ABC's in this book can enhance your self-esteem. Give careful consideration to the affirmations, exercises and actions at the end of each chapter and make them a part of your daily routine. You will begin to notice a difference. But nothing will change until you decide to take action. So start now! As you do, approach it with the idea of having fun. This is important for your happiness as well as your self-esteem.

I believe it is obvious by now that I am a firm believer in having fun, and writing this book was no exception. It was truly a labor of love. I sincerely hope that was apparent through these pages. My fondest wish, though, is that you have found this book inspiring and entertaining to read, practical to use and, when used, does make a difference in your life. I invite you to call or write to let me know of your successes. Until then, **MAKE** yourself a great day and may God bless! I leave you with these thoughts on the **ABC's of Self-Esteem:**

THE A B C's OF SELF-ESTEEM

The person with high self-esteem has a positive **A**ttitude. It stems from **B**elief in oneself and belief in God our Creator. It comes to the one who combines **C**onfidence and **D**ecision-making with **E**nthusiasm and **F**aith — faith in oneself, in others and in God. He sets **G**oals and pursues them vigorously with **H**onesty and **I**magination. **J**oy fills his life because of the **K**indness and **L**ove he shares with others. He serves as a role **M**odel for those around him by **N**urturing the growth and development of self, family and friends. His **O**ptimism is used in striving to reach his **P**otential and to live a **Q**uality life. He readily accepts **R**esponsibility for his actions and renders valuable **S**ervice to his profession and community. His **T**alents are used to bring about **U**nderstanding among people in order to ensure peace and harmony in the world. He **V**isualizes the best in himself and others and always sees **W**orth and dignity in all human beings. His **X**pectations are high but fair and reasonable. He **Y**earns for success and pursues it relentlessly with zest and **Z**eal. He is a pleasure to be around and a delight to see. With God's help, today, that person will be me.

ABOUT THE AUTHOR

Curt Boudreaux is a professional speaker and author. He received a B.S. from Nicholls State University in Thibodaux, Louisiana and a Masters +30 degree in guidance and counseling from Ole Miss.

He was in education for twenty-four years and served as principal of Golden Meadow Middle School for ten. In 1988 he was honored as a National Distinguished Principal. This award is jointly sponsored by the U.S. Department of Education and the National Association of Elementary School Principals to recognize excellence in school administration. Only one public school principal from each state is selected annually for this award.

Curt is a member of the National Speakers Association and is immediate past president of the New Orleans Chapter. He is also past Chairman of the Board of the South Lafourche Chamber of Commerce and is presently serving as Chairman of the Board of Commissioners of Lady of The Sea Hospital.

He is a ten year veteran of prison ministry work and is a volunteer in the Kairos Prison Ministry at Louisiana State Penitentiary at Angola.

Curt "retired" from education seven years ago to pursue a career in professional speaking. He does keynotes, seminars and workshops throughout the country addressing the topics of self-esteem, attitude, inspiration, and human relations.

He is a developer of people and focuses on the "human side of quality." He inspires individuals, educators and company employees to feel good about themselves and develop their potential. Each presentation is designed to inform, entertain and inspire. His Cajun sense of humor, enthusiasm and passion for speaking combined with strong presentation skills enable him to relate easily to audiences and effectively communicate his message.

Curt and his wife, Sue, live in the small community of Cut Off, Louisiana, along the banks of Bayou Lafourche. This Cajun speaks from the heart! Let him speak to yours! Should you be interested in Curt speaking to your group or ordering additional books, you may contact:

Curt Boudreaux
P.O. Box 422
Golden Meadow, LA 70357
985-632-6177
985-632-4898 - FAX

PROGRAM TITLES

- The ABC's of Self-Esteem
- The Keys to Unlocking Your Potential
- The Human Side of Quality
- You Only Go Around Once
- The Art of Leadership
- Winning Attitudes

ORDER FORM

THE ABC'S OF SELF-ESTEEM: A PRACTICAL APPROACH (Book) Price: $21.50 per book. (Tax Included) Add postage/shipping costs at the rate of $2.00 for the first book and $1.00 for each additional book.

"THE KEYS TO UNLOCKING YOUR POTENTIAL" (Audio tape) Price: $10.75 per tape. (Tax Included) Add postage/shipping costs at the rate of $1.00 for the first tape and $ .50 for each additional tape.

_____**books** at $21.50 per book . . . _______
Postage/shipping costs . . . . . _______

_____**audio tapes** at $10.75 per tape _______
Postage/shipping costs . . . . . _______

Total amount enclosed . . . . . ._______

Make check or money order payable to Curt Boudreaux and send to:

Curt Boudreaux
P.O. Box 422
Golden Meadow, LA 70357
985-632-6177 FAX: 985-632-4898

- -

Name:_________________________Telephone( )___________
Address: ______________________________________
City: ______________________State_______Zip___________
Please send information to me on the following:
____**THE ABC'S OF SELF-ESTEEM: A PRACTICAL APPROACH** Audio Cassette Album
____ Details about Curt Boudreaux speaking to my group.